KILLING HYDRA

BREAKING THE CYCLE OF BLOODLINE AND SELF-INFLICTED CURSES

RHONDA CROSSMAN

FOREWORD BY TIFFANY BLACKWELL

CONTENTS

FOREWORD

Rhonda Crossman is a servant on fire for God! Jesus is her consuming desire! She's been through some things and has keen discernment. This latest book of hers had me in tears at key moments! How I wish that *Killing Hydra* was available in my formative years. Truly, a lot of heartache could have been spared, with freedom bells clearing the atmosphere around me.

If you've ever been involved in witchcraft, had family members who were (or are), then this book is a TOOL for demolishing the strongholds and demonic altars of the enemy over your life! If you are new to the prophetic or to Christianity (your relationship with Jesus), keep reading *Killing Hydra* with an open heart and mind. This book is anointed to break and crush invisible demonic heads that have opposed you for a long time.

You will feel invigorated and your desire to continue your journey in Christ will return. As I read this, I could see and feel God's presence remove chains from minds and hearts, remove veils from eyes and the unstopping of spiritual ears!

I appreciate the privilege and honor to communicate on the breaker anointing that is on this book! Lastly, I want to encourage you to allow Holy Spirit to work within you as situations and scenarios are brought to the surface. Receive your healing!

Jesus, we thank You for the transformative power of Your Spirit that will touch everyone who touches or reads Killing Hydra! May your knowledge contained in this book set the masses free!

Rhonda has sought the Lord diligently for answers regarding warfare, demonic cycles, struggles, familiar spirits, and so much more! The Lord did not disappoint. This book will keep you engaged and have your attention the whole way through! Literally, the wind and breath of God will carry you along. Go journey and heal with Jesus.... enjoy.

Tiffany Blackwell

Charity Founder of Tiffany Blackwell Ministries

Mississippi, USA

Review

Many of us are searching for truth, but we are still bound, or we are too blinded by pridefulness to see the strongholds of the spiritual world or to acknowledge its unapologetic restrictions on our lives, families, and bloodlines.

Rhonda has a profound gift of insight into the spiritual world and is a prophetic voice for today's perilous times. She has been a blessing and a wonderful friend who offers wisdom, compassion, and guidance as we navigate this complicated unseen spiritual reality, which is more real than the physical world.

Rhonda has sought guidance from the Lord in every endeavor of writing and in conjunction with the Holy Spirit delivers a masterfully designed window into the spiritual reality that most of us are unaware. In the pages of this book, you will gain an invaluable understanding of spiritual matters and the power to overcome the Hydra spirit you face.

Seeking knowledge and understanding of the legal rights your ancestors have granted access to over your bloodline, your life and prayerfully removing these unseen ties will give you and your family in generations to come the freedom to walk in your God-given destiny and authority. This freedom cannot be understated but a lack of knowledge will keep you and generations in bondage. If you are reading this, you are the lineage to free your bloodline from bondage.

It is a great honor to read the pages of this book, reflect on the teachings and gain the understanding that allows us the authority to destroy the Hydra spirit in our lives, and our bloodlines. These teachings will afford protection to our future generations to walk with grace in their God-given authority and destiny.

Steven Fredrick Roushar

Fire & Gas Lead Technician

Wasilla, Alaska, USA

PREFACE

I wrote *Killing Hydra* because the Holy Spirit impressed upon me to look at my generational and bloodline issues to address those pesty things that remain and show themselves from time to time as well as assist those within and outside of my family with unraveling themselves from generational curses. Psalm 51:5 ESV says, *"Behold, I was brought forth in iniquity, and in sin did my mother conceive me."* Iniquity implies being wicked or immoral in character and nature. We all have generational iniquity of some sort. And if not our own, we are paying for the sins of our fathers.

We all have two parents, four grandparents, eight great grandparents, and it doubles as we continue to count backwards. And since all have sinned, that's a lot of iniquity coming through the bloodline and ultimately a lot of reasons for the enemy to create blockades and hindrances legally in our life and the lives of generations that proceed from us.

Killing Hydra reinforces the fact that generational issues cannot and should not be ignored. Dealing with generational issues is like taking a detox. I cannot be eating junk food all my life or periodically and then suddenly begin eating healthy and assume that I am healthy automatically.

Where did all the toxins go from my unhealthy time of eating? Nowhere. The toxins will not go anywhere until addressed directly by way of a detox. We cannot build a healthy structure on an unhealthy foundation. This is why many people are saved yet they are having the same issues as their unsaved family members or relatives. Unhealthy foundations need to be dug up and destroyed and a new foundation needs to be built. We dig up and rebuild a healthy foundation when we address bloodline issues directly.

In addition to bloodline issues, we have iniquities of our own that the enemy uses as legal grounds to heap hindrances in our path. The enemy is relentless; hence, we should give no place to him. The spirit of Hydra is responsible for creating and maintaining negative cycles and recurrences in people's lives and bloodlines.

I wrote *Killing Hydra* with great simplicity so that everyone, everywhere can read it and understand the importance of removing the Hydra from their bloodline.

Hydra

"He will make an utter end of it. Affliction will not rise up a second time."
Nahum 1:9b NKJV

What is Hydra?

According to Greek mythology, a Hydra is a gigantic snakelike water monster with two to nine heads, one of which was considered immortal. This monster was known to contaminate fresh water by releasing poisonous gasses from its mouth. It was also said to surface from the seas' depths periodically to harm people and their livestock.

Anyone who attempted to behead the Hydra discovered quickly that two heads emerged from the freshly cut wound. As a result, killing the creature was laborious and required a two-person team—one person to cut off the head while the other cauterized the fresh wound so that a new head would not emerge.

A crab was assigned to assist the Hydra in defeating its adversary, but the crab was crushed without being of any assistance, and all the heads of the

Hydra were cut off. The immortal head was buried under a huge rock to prevent it from doing harm since it would not die like the mortal heads.

The legend has it that the one who slayed the beast dipped his arrows in the monster's poisonous blood to inflict wounds on others, but unfortunately that caused his accidental death at the hands of his wife.

Make It Relatable

Rather than debating on whether the myth was true, I will use it as a touchpoint to tell the story of our lives, because in so many ways it is a powerful replica of the spiritual reality that most of us face. We've all had negative experiences, but sometimes the same negative experience seems to reoccur repeatedly. Even if we change our environment or circumstances, it feels like we are living through the same cycle or pattern of a particular negative trend. It could be cycles of poor relationships, a pattern of having your heart broken by romantic partners, attracting toxic or narcissistic romantic partners, acquiring things of value only to lose it all, or at the moment that you solve a particular problem, another one shows up.

Aside from negative patterns showing up in an individual's life, there could be negative patterns occurring in a family or bloodline, such as early death, death at a certain age, divorce, addictions, mental health issues, children born outside of marriage, poor marital relationships, miscarriages, generational sickness, poor education, poverty, stagnation in your career, unemployment, or underemployment. This is by no means exhaustive but dealing with them and other manifestations of negative reoccurrences can make life feel like hard labor. If you have not observed any negative reoccurring pattern in your life or bloodline already, begin to reflect and observe. Upon observation, you will notice the negative reoccurring patterns. Every individual and every bloodline has these patterns. These patterns are evidence that you are dealing with a Hydra spirit. Hydra is real; it is a demonic entity. Hydra is the spirit responsible for negative recurrences, negative patterns and negative cycles.

Let's Examine the Myth

The legend mentioned that the Hydra harmed people and livestock – which was their source of provision. Today we would translate livestock to jobs, businesses, and other sources of income. This means that the Hydra afflicted the individual on every level - spiritually, mentally, physically, financially, and socially.

The Hydra's immortal head. The Hydra's immortal head informs us that the source of the negative recurrences is spiritual in nature. It's anchored in the dark spiritual realm. Negative cycles and patterns are always spiritual in nature. The enemy wants to keep us and our bloodline spinning in negativity and stagnation, but Jesus Christ is that Rock that crushes the immortal head of the Hydra. We do not have to live in the fear that we are powerless against the spiritual roots of personal and generational patterns and cycles.

The Hydra's many heads. The mythical creature is said to have two to nine heads. When we reflect on our bloodline and casualties that we brought on ourselves, we will recognize that opportunities were created for the Hydra to grow many heads. It's never just one thing. Sin has consequences, but not all sin carries the same weight; not all sin results in curses. Nevertheless, the consequences that are weighty and the sins that bring curses are usually put into effect by different actions and choices, resulting in the many-headed monster that we face today.

This monster was known to contaminate fresh water by releasing poisonous gasses from its mouth. Matthew 12:37 ESV says, *"For by your words you will be justified, and by your words you will be condemned."* Proverbs 18:21 ESV tells us, *"Death and life are in the power of the tongue, and those who love it will eat its fruits."* Unless someone is controlled by demons, no one—human or demon—can make them say things they don't want to say. Demons can use hardships, frustrations, weariness, and discouragement as opportunities to influence an individual into making negative confessions and releasing word curses into their own lives and into the lives of their children.

This is why it is wiser to remain silent when you are in a negative mental or emotional state. The devil is opportunistic; refuse to have him use you against yourself. Do not be stirred into releasing poisonous gasses into your fresh water. Sometimes when people have negative experiences, instead of rebuking the demon influencing the negative situations, they will say things like, "This always happens to me," or, "Just my luck." That's how the enemy tricks people into doing his dirty work of contaminating their fresh water and locking themselves in negative cycles. In 1 Kings 19:4 the enemy wearied the prophet Elijah to the point that he concluded that he was no better than his ancestors. This is not a confession that we want to make. We are better! We are breaking out, and we are breaking through, regardless of what it looks like or feels like.

Hydra was raised to kill. John 10:10 NKJV says, *"The thief does not come except to steal, and to kill, and to destroy. I have come that they may have life, and that they may have it more abundantly."* The assignment of the devil and his demons will always be destructive in nature. The enemy will steal from you, whether its things that are tangible—like possessions and opportunities, or intangible things, like peace and joy. What the enemy cannot steal, he will destroy; you will have it, but it will be of no use. This is why certain relationships are filled with torment and terror; the individual is in it but they cannot enjoy it.

Other times, he goes for the kill. The devil can manipulate situations and circumstances in an individual's life to the point that they fall into a state of depression and hopelessness and conclude that taking their own life is the only way out. In some situations, the devil has no legal grounds to kill, whether it's through sickness, diseases or accidents, so he manipulates the individual into doing it. This is the type of manipulation that results in some people committing suicide. Abortion is another way in which the enemy goes for the kill, but he gets the individual to do his dirty work.

The Hydra's beheaded heads regrew. The regrowing of the Hydra's head is a sign of unbroken curses and ignored negative individual and generational patterns and cycles. On the other hand, self-inflicted and negative generational patterns do not go away with one prayer, or in one deliverance session. First, we must want to be free of the negative patterns and cycles. Second, we must be consistent in our pursuit to be free, whether it's by prayer and fasting, or by how we speak and live, or both. We need to stand flat-footed and face our Hydra.

And if we truly want to be free and remain free, we need to break free of the "pray for me" mentality. Some people like to contract out their prayer lives. They are always looking for someone to pray for them. The smallest sound of "boo" from the devil will have them chasing after someone to pray for them. We have to learn to speak back to the enemy. Let him know the sound of our voice and let him see us standing in our authority. Authority is not volume – in how loud we speak. In its simplest form, authority is standing on your right to say "no" to the enemy.

When you deal with a negative personal or generational pattern and you see it attempting to raise its head again, cut it off. We must stand firm because the enemy will test our resolve. We will behead the Hydra completely over a period of time, but it does not have to be a prolonged period. It all comes down to how badly you want to be free. Be more relentless than the enemy; outlast him. Sometimes when God delivers you from one thing, another thing surfaces. Handle it as it arises. We can never be freed from everything all at once. Stay the course and endure the process. Your victory is your responsibility. You gain authority over the demons you defeat.

"Again I say to you, if two of you agree on earth about anything they ask, it will be done for them by my Father in heaven." Matthew 18:19 ESV

<u>Defeating the Hydra required a two-person team.</u> There is power in agreement. We can never have it all figured out. Sometimes we need people to pray for us and with us. Sometimes we need people to fast for us and with us. Sometimes we need advice and counseling. Sometimes we need therapy. Whatever form the assistance takes, we will always need the assistance of others to defeat the Hydra in our lives. For this reason, we need to ask God to lead us to the right people or send the right people our way. It's also important to use discernment, especially in this time when there is an increase of false apostles, prophets, evangelists, pastors, teachers and deliverance ministers. The devil is spitting out counterfeits.

Sometimes the situation is challenging and people are desperate. In the midst of desperation, discernment is critical. Pray for discernment and ask God to protect you from deception. None of us is above being deceived, and sometimes desperation and brokenness dulls our discernment. It's important to have spiritual leaders in our lives whom we trust, and it's important to use wisdom instead of chasing after the newest influential social media preacher. There is the good, the bad and the indifferent on social media. While we are alive we will need people, and God will use people to help us along the way.

On the other hand, we should not idolize people. Sometimes believers develop the church version of Stockholm syndrome with a Christian leader or deliverance minister who played an important or significant role in their life. While showing honor, loyalty and appreciation is biblical and important, developing unhealthy soul ties with someone whom God used to help you is not good or godly. We applaud and celebrate the gifted and anointed, but ultimately the highest honor and glory goes to God the Father, God the Son, and God the Holy Spirit, the Giver of the gift, the gifted and the anointing. It is a sin to idolize people. Don't stalk deliverance ministers from event to event hoping to get their attention.

Some Christians have developed an addiction to deliverance. They are always looking for the next deliverance event. Some Christians need deliverance from their addiction to deliverance. Deliverance is a process, and the casting out of demons is only a part of it. The major responsibility as it relates to deliverance lies with the believer. It is your responsibility to seek deliverance, and to have the demons cast out. Also, it is your responsibility to maintain your deliverance. You need to keep the demons out by changing your lifestyle—the behaviors and mindset that gave the demons access in the first place. The casting out of demons is just one aspect of deliverance. Once that's done, the deliverance minister did his or her part; now you need to do your part. Do not become a clean but unoccupied house. Demons see humans as their house. When the demons are cast out, do not leave the house unoccupied. Fill the house with God and grow spiritually.

<u>A crab was assigned to assist the Hydra in defeating its adversary.</u>
The crab spirit is associated with a competitive and comparative way of thinking and living. Crabs do not assist each other; instead they pull each other down or try to climb over each other to get to the top. When the Hydra is assisted by a crab spirit it only serves to strengthen negative cycles and keep the victim frustrated. There can be people with the crab spirit in families, and among friends and associates. There will always be people who are more concerned about counting your blessings and breakthroughs more than they count theirs. Such people are filled with envy, jealousy, strife, and slander. They are committed to doing whatever it takes to pull you down in an attempt to fulfill their dream of rising above you. Such people will always seek to control the narrative of your life.

Crabs are crustaceans. The word "crustacean" originated from the Latin word, "crusta," meaning "hard shell." This describes people with the crab spirit well. They usually don't stop to think that working together may get things in motion faster and create lasting results that can be beneficial to all concerned. Rather, like crabs, they have a hard exterior, but intelligent discourse is not happening internally. From that place of not being thinkers, they set out to crush the vision, plans, and destinies of others, sometimes to their own detriment. Also, since crabs tend to have nothing much on the interior of their hard shell, the devil usually fills such people with negative ways of thinking. The mindset of the people around you can keep your life in negative and demonic cycles and prevent you from fulfilling your God-ordained destiny. For this reason, you cannot allow yourself to feel obligated in any way to such people. People who are bound in their thinking cannot bring you into freedom.

Lastly, the crab spirit is associated with demonic mind control. Both Hydra and the Crab spirit are marine demons. Marine demons specialize in mind control. Proverbs 23:7a NKJV says, *"For as he thinks in his heart, so is he."* There are demons assigned to control the mindset and ways of thinking of individuals and families to keep them in the bondages of demonic patterns and cycles. The mindset and way of thinking has to be changed on an individual level to crush the crab spirit and break demonic patterns and cycles effectively in your personal life or that which came down generationally. Your mind must be renewed continuously.

It Shall Not Arise A Second Time

Although the cycle of Hydra is real, for the believers of the Lord Jesus Christ, according to Nahum 1:9, the same affliction is not supposed to arise in our lives a second time. From this, we understand that negative recurrences and cycles are not to be expected or accepted as normal, and demonic patterns are not to be permitted. God does not want the lives of those who belong to Him to be characterized and plagued by cycles of sufferings and distress. This is not to say that we will not have to endure testing, trials or experience hardships; of course we will. 2 Timothy 2:3 NKJV tells us, *"You therefore must endure hardship as a good soldier of Jesus Christ."*

It is important that we differentiate between the testing, trials, and hardships that a believer in Christ must face versus individual and generational distress and cycles. Testing, trials, and hardships happen to believers of Christ, not to your bloodline or generation. It does not happen to your family members unless they are believers also. The devil hates those who belong to Christ, so he will try to make their lives unpleasant, and God will allow those who belong to Him to be tested and tried so that they grow and mature in every way. Individual and generational distress, on the other hand, reduces and diminishes an individual or bloodline. For the born-again believer, this cycle has no authority to continue.

"Therefore, if anyone is in Christ, he is a new creation; old things have passed away; behold, all things have become new." 2 Corinthians 5:17 NKJV

Although negative cycles and patterns are not authorized, authority must be exercised. Victory is not automatic; it must be enforced. On an individual level, every believer will have to stand in the authority given to them by Christ Jesus over individual and bloodline distress and cycles and break the power of the enemy. I will say this in another way to reinforce it: victory is not automatic. If it were, then the moment someone gave their life to Christ the negative cycles and patterns would have stopped immediately. They did not stop immediately because the individual needs to enforce their authority deliberately and directly and lay claim to the new life that Christ has to offer and everything that goes with it.

"Behold, I have given you authority to tread on serpents and scorpions, and over all the power of the enemy, and nothing shall hurt you." Luke 10:19 ESV

Believers in Christ were not given power or authority over some of the power of the enemy, we were given power and authority over ALL the power of the enemy. Every believer in Christ is empowered to cancel bloodline distress and cycles completely. We have what it takes to kill Hydra and crush that crustacean that comes with it.

Prayer to Break Generational Patterns and Distress

Heavenly Father, Your Word in Nahum 1:9 NKJV says, "He will make an utter end of it. Affliction will not rise up a second time." In the name of Jesus Christ, I renounce, I fall out of agreement with, and I cancel the power of generational distress, negative patterns and cycles in my life, in the lives of my children and in the generations that will come after me. I disallow the afflictions, curses, frustrations, hardships, difficulties, challenges, financial struggles, infirmities, distress, traumas, and dramas that were on my father and his bloodline and on my mother and her bloodline from coming upon me, my children, and generations that come from me. I stand in the authority that Christ Jesus gave me, and I slay the Hydra that I gave spiritual access. I also slay the Hydra of my ancestors. I cancel the assignment of every Hydra raised against my life. I bring an utter end to it now, in Jesus' name.

In the name of Jesus Christ, I break the power and agreement of demonic mind control, influence, and manipulation against my mind, the minds of my children, and the generations that will come from me.

In the name of Jesus Christ, I sever all connections between myself and the marine kingdom. I sever all connections between my children and the marine kingdom. I tear down all altars. I end all covenants, agreements, oaths, vows, and marriages made knowingly and unknowingly by me, by my children, and by my ancestors with the marine kingdom.

In the name of Jesus Christ, I break down every altar in the marine kingdom that's speaking against my life, against the lives of my children, and against my bloodline. I close every vortex and seal them shut with the blood of Jesus Christ. I plead the blood of Jesus Christ around myself, my children, and my bloodline. I decree that the blood of Jesus Christ forms a barrier between us and the marine kingdom.

In the name of Jesus Christ, I decree that the marine kingdom will not be able to exercise illegitimate authority and influence over my life, over the lives of my children and over the generations that will come from me.

I sever the power of the crab spirit and I cast down the crab mentality from my mind, from the minds of my children and from future generations after me. I declare that we have the mind of Christ.

Jesus Christ, My Lord, My Rock, I ask that You crush the immortal head of the Hydra in my life, in the lives of my children and in my bloodline; let it never rise again.

In the name of Jesus Christ, I release the fire of God to burn up all the heads of the Hydra completely, and I command all the Hydra's watery places in my life, in the lives of my children and in my bloodline to become dry.

I command spirits of generational afflictions and curses to come out of my life now, in the name of Jesus Christ.

I command spirits of generational infirmities and diseases to come out of my life now, in the name of Jesus Christ.

I command spirits of generational poverty, lack, and financial struggles to come out of my life now, in the name of Jesus Christ.

I command spirits of generational distress, trauma, and drama to come out of my life now, in the name of Jesus Christ.

I command spirits associated with generational frustrations, hardships, difficulties, and challenges, to come out of my life now, in the name of Jesus Christ.

I decree that I belong to Jesus Christ. I decree that my children belong to Jesus Christ. I decree that the generations that come from me belong to Jesus Christ. Jesus Christ is our Lord. I decree that we are the Lord's portion, His people, and His inheritance. I decree, according to Isaiah 61:3 ESV, the Lord Jesus Christ gives us beauty instead of ashes, the oil of gladness instead of mourning, the garment of praise instead of a faint spirit. I decree that we are called oaks of righteousness, and the planting of the Lord that He may be glorified.

I come into agreement with 2 Corinthians 5:17 NKJV, that says, "Therefore, if anyone is in Christ, he is a new creation; old things have passed away; behold, all things have become new." I decree new things in my life. I decree new things in the lives of my children, and I decree new things in the lives of those who will come after us.

I decree that according to Psalm 1:1-3 ESV, we are blessed. We do not walk in the counsel of the wicked, nor stand in the way of sinners, nor sit in the seat of scoffers; but our delight is in the law of the Lord, and on his law, we meditate day and night. I decree that we are like trees planted by streams of water; we yield fruit in its season, and our leaves do not wither. I decree that whatever we put our hands to do prospers. In the mighty name of Jesus Christ, Amen.

GENERATIONAL CURSES

"...so the curse causeless shall not come." Proverbs 26:2 KJV

Recurring negative patterns always indicate that a curse is present. The curse causeless shall not come, meaning it can do you no harm. With curses there is always a reason, a cause. It's important to find out what caused the curse and deal with it. The cause can vary from person to person. The most common sources of curses are embedded in the rebellion and iniquity of our ancestors.

Exodus 34:7 KJV: *"Keeping mercy for thousands, forgiving iniquity and transgression and sin, and that will by no means clear the guilty; visiting the iniquity of the fathers upon the children, and upon the children's children, unto the third and to the fourth generation."*

There are generational blessings and generational curses. It is important that we observe our bloodline prayerfully and discover what are blessings so that we can nurture and come into agreement with them and what are curses so that we can cut them off and break agreement with them. Generational blessings could be wealth, longevity, good health, talent and creativity, good education, good family relationships, lasting marriages, faith in Christ, and the like. In 2 Timothy 1:5 the young man was commended for his sincere faith; it was mentioned that the same faith was in his mother and grandmother. This is an example of a generational blessing. Generational curses are the negative patterns and trends in the bloodline. Since this book is about killing Hydra, we will focus on handling curses.

Curse: To injure; to subject to evil, to vex, harass or torment with great calamities.[1]

A negative generational pattern of behavior indicates that a curse is present, or it will lead to a curse. An example of a negative generational pattern of behavior is with Abraham, Isaac and Jacob. They all used deception to navigate difficult situations. Both Abraham and Isaac lied, claiming that their wives were their sisters, because they feared for their lives. Jacob was sneaky with Laban. Some family have similar negative behaviors such as lying, stealing, anger and rage, swearing, being prideful, being lustful, being adulterous, and so on. Some negative patterns of behaviors are not necessarily curses, but these patterns of behaviors frequently accommodate choices and decisions that create the causes for curses.

God's Justice System

Whether we are believers or not, we pay for the sins of our fathers to the third and fourth generations if they sinned and rebelled against God. Any act of sinning against God is an act of rebellion, and depending on the nature of their sin, we suffer. Every human is presented with opportunities daily to obey or disobey God's commandments. There are blessings for obedience and curses for disobedience; Deuteronomy chapter 28 indicates these principles clearly. The Word of God are laws in the realm of the spirit. Like the laws in any nation, the laws of God protect those who respect and obey them and punishes those who disrespect and disobey them. It's like any legal and justice system that is aligned fairly and morally. God has a legal and justice system too, and everything He created, both in the seen and unseen realms, fall under the jurisdiction of that system.

As it relates to God's legal and justice system, it's never a matter of God's love for us; it's a matter of how the systems work that were set up by God. His love for us would not lead Him to violate the systems that He set up. In this aspect, He is fair and just to us, and He is fair and just to Satan, the enemy. Let's suppose your father is a judge of a Supreme Court; if you violate—let's say, the traffic laws—you will get a ticket or fine. If you kill someone, you will be charged accordingly. The law is obligated to punish you, and this has nothing to do with your father's love for you. Your offense put you in the jurisdiction of the law of the land, not in the love of your father. Your father loves you and will try to get you the best lawyer, but the legal and justice system must handle your situation, not your daddy's love. It's the same with God, our heavenly Father. We need to be clear about this dynamic at all times.

Generationally, the legal and justice system that God established impacts us based on the choices made by our ancestors. If there are signs that our life is under a curse, then our ancestors had disobeyed and rebelled against God. They did not serve Him; they did not keep covenant with Him. Their disobedience and rebellion will result in both them and their future generations enduring curses consequently. In this instance, the curses are the judgment of God.

Hydra Wants to Stay

The Hydra demon in the bloodline could also try to influence the next generation into committing acts of rebellion against God so that it can remain in the bloodline. Bloodline simply means generation or family. Based on Scripture, after or at the fourth generation, Satan and his demonic host can no longer afflict anyone legally for sins of their ancestors. The legal right to the bloodline has come to an end once the children of the rebellious parents did not continue in their parents' rebellion. This does not mean that the Hydra will not try to remain illegitimately or illegally. Although Satan is legalistic, he's neither fair nor just. But we have an advocate with the Father, as stated in 1 John 2:1. An advocate is a lawyer. Jesus is our Lawyer in the spiritual legal and justice system. God, our Heavenly Father, has already solicited Jesus Christ to fight on our behalf. Our role is to cooperate with our Lawyer.

Break The Curse

"You shall have no other gods before Me." Exodus 20:3 NKJV

Make no mistake, you will have to break off bloodline curses from your life because of the sins of your parents and ancestors. Do not fall into the error of misunderstanding Galatians 3:13 NKJV that says, *"Christ has redeemed us from the curse of the law, having become a curse for us (for it is written, "Cursed is everyone who hangs on a tree")."* Jesus was hung on a tree. The curse that Christ faced is the curse of the law. The Scripture was very specific. During the time that Christ was on earth, the people lived according to the laws of Moses, and under those laws they were required to offer animal sacrifices for their sins. They had to obey other national restrictions and religious formalities as well.

There were different types of laws.

Civil Laws: This category of law was given to ancient Israel under the Theocracy of God. God was the Leader and Ruler of the entire nation. This was a nation that God chose for Himself, so He set their laws. This category included laws that required witches and men who had sexual relations with other men to be stoned. Since we are no longer under the Theocracy of God but are under other systems of government, witches and homosexuals cannot be dragged out in the open and stoned.

Ceremonial Laws: This category included animal sacrifices, purity and ritual cleansing. This is the category of law that Jesus addressed when He became a curse by hanging on a tree. We are no longer required to offer animal sacrifices for sins. If we do this, we will be denying the sacrifice that Jesus made when He died on the tree once and for all humanity. Galatians 3:13 was referring to the sacrifice that Jesus made when He became a sacrifice on the tree. We are no longer obligated to live under the burden of these laws.

Moral Laws: This category of laws always applies to us. The moral laws tell us how we are allowed to live and how we are not allowed to live. This category includes sexual sins and the like. If we, or our ancestors, break laws in this category, Satan and his team, including Hydra, have legal rights to enter and afflict the bloodline.

The Laws of Allegiance. I added this category. The first and second commandments are what I refer to as the laws of allegiance. The Creator of heaven and earth does not want us to be in allegiance, agreement, or to worship other gods. We are not to worship: idols, fallen angels, marine deities, demons, or aliens. Aliens fall into the category of fallen angels and other demonic entities. We are not to make covenants with any of them, nor are we to build altars to them. We are not to be in allegiance or agreement with them in any way. We are not to make for ourselves gods or idols. It's completely forbidden. Disobeying God in this regard is an act of rebellion and will result in curses in the bloodline.

"I am the Lord your God, who brought you out of the land of Egypt, out of the house of slavery. You shall have no other gods before me. You shall not make for yourself a carved image, or any likeness of anything that is in heaven above, or that is in the earth beneath, or that is in the water under the earth. You shall not bow down to them or serve them, for I the Lord your God am a jealous God, visiting the iniquity of the fathers on the children to the third and fourth generation of those who hate me..." Exodus 20: 2 -5 ESV.

Of the categories of laws mentioned above, Christ only redeemed us from the second category – the ceremonial laws. The first category is no longer in effect because we are not a global Theocracy, instead, every nation has its own laws. The two latter categories are still in effect. Breaking laws in those categories will result in generational curses. Note that God considers rebellion against Him as hate. But all is not lost; we can repent on behalf of our ancestors.

Before we repent on behalf of our ancestors, let's ensure that all are in right relationship with God. I don't want to assume that everyone reading this book is in right relationship with God. Furthermore, it's dangerous to break generational curses and then return to living in rebellion to God. If you do that, your life will be seven times worse than it was before, which is undesirable. In addition to that, the promises and blessings of God are for those who are in right relationship with Him.

1 John 1:9 ESV says, *"If we confess our sins, he is faithful and just to forgive us our sins and to cleanse us from all unrighteousness."*

If you have never accepted Jesus Christ as the Lord of your life, I encourage you to do so now.

Pray this prayer: *"Heavenly Father, I come to You in the name of Jesus Christ, Your dear Son. I believe that Jesus died for my sins, and I believe that He rose from the dead. I believe that He is seated in Heavenly places with You right now. I repent of every way that I sinned against you in thoughts, words, or deeds. I ask that you forgive my sins and pardon my iniquities. I confess and accept Him as Lord of my life. I invite the Holy Spirit to come and live in my heart right now. Amen."*

If you said this prayer, I pray that you become, and remain, firmly planted in Christ. I pray that you do and become all that God has created you to be and do. I pray that you enjoy the rewards and blessings of being in right relationship with Christ. I pray that God connects you to people who will help you grow in Him, in Jesus' name, Amen. I welcome you to the family of God.

Before we move on to discuss the rebellion of our ancestors, have you noticed that in the myth it says that the Hydra is a water monster and it surfaced periodically to bring harm? Water can imply two things: firstly, generation. Your father's sperm was liquid; it's water, but of a different composition. That means you were liquid before you became solid. So, the Hydra could have been connected to you from your father's or forefathers' loins. Secondly, water here implies a marine or water spirit. We will treat the Hydra as both. So, the Hydra is a marine spirit that came through the bloodline.

Let us repent of the rebellion of our ancestors.

Heavenly Father, in the name of Jesus Christ, I come to You to repent on behalf of my ancestors' rebellion from both parents' generations. (If you are aware of some of the sins that your parents and fore-parents committed, please mention them here; if not, say) I am sorry and I repent of every way in which they sinned against, rebelled against, and offended You. I refuse, reject, renounce, and divorce myself from their sins, their agreements, their covenants, their altars, their idols, every spirit in the air, on the land, in the sea, and every other place that are connected to their sins, their covenants, their agreements, their altars and idols, and their familiar spirits. I want no part of it. I release the blood of Jesus Christ to my foundation, and I ask that the blood of Jesus Christ now redeem and deliver me, my children and bloodline from every evil altar, covenant, agreement, Satanic hindrance, blockage, and curse placed on my life and on my bloodline. Deliver me from every familiar spirit that is attached to my bloodline, in Jesus' mighty name, Amen.

Breaking Generational Patterns

It's one thing to break generational curses, but it's just as important to break generational patterns. Generational patterns have to do with mind-sets, ways of thinking and living, behaviors and habits of the family. These patterns can be passed down from generation to generation because families learn behaviors from each other, whether good or bad. This creates a safe house or stronghold for whatever is carried in the bloodline, whether they are blessings or curses. It's important that we unlearn the negative generational ways of thinking—whether it's about God, ourselves, other people, or life in general, and unravel from negative generational patterns. We need to destroy the safe houses and strongholds where demons, including Hydra, hide out. We can cast the demon out, but if the house still exists, the demons will lurk and wait for opportunities to return.

Deliverance and discipleship are important keys. Never think that you don't need deliverance. Everyone needs deliverance. The thought that a Christian cannot have a demon is a lie from the pit of hell. I was saved for many years, and I still go through periodic deliverance. I am a firm believer in receiving the ministry of deliverance. We are ignorant about all kinds of things within our bloodline, and what you don't know can hurt you and hinder your progress in life. Additionally, we pick up things along the way. If you have been through difficult or traumatic experiences —for example, you ended a relationship with a narcissist, or you were in some other type of abusive relationship or situation, or you got divorced, then you need to address the residue of those experiences through deliverance. One of the reasons why people complain of cycles is that they never got delivered from what harmed them during life, so it recurs. Deliverance removes the demonic occupant from the house, i.e., your life.

Discipleship is another important factor. The only way to guarantee no return is to demolish the house. Discipleship demolishes the safe house of the enemy in your life. We achieve this by renewing our minds daily with the Word of God. Joshua 1:8 tells us to meditate on the Word of God day and night. Biblical meditation means to read and ponder on the Word of God.

You don't have to read the entire Bible all at once. Read a verse of Scripture or a few, think about what you read, and look up meanings of words in those verses of Scripture, if necessary. It's even better if you can set aside a quiet place and time to do this. In Psalm 119:11 NIV the Psalmist said, "I have hidden your word in my heart that I might not sin against you." Hide the Scripture that you meditated on in your heart and apply it to everyday living. That's how you destroy the stronghold of any generational demon. As for the Hydra, the presence of the Word of God in your life will dry up the waters so that it will no longer be able to hide.

Suffering and Sins of the Fathers

"Prepare slaughter for his children for the iniquity of their fathers..." Isaiah 14:21 KJV

King David in the Bible is a good example of children suffering because of the sins of their father. David lusted after and then had an affair with Bathsheba, the wife of Uriah. Bathsheba became pregnant as a result of this affair. When King David's plan to pin the pregnancy on Uriah did not work, he had Uriah killed. His actions created a cause for a curse, and the curse took effect in the lives of his children - Amnon, Absalom and Tamar.

His son Amnon lured his young half-sister Tamar, who was a virgin, into his house by pretending to be sick and needing her assistance. When Tamar came to assist him, he raped her and then threw her out. Their father did nothing about it. Tamar's brother Absalom, who shared both mother and father with her, was angry about it but said nothing. Two years later he killed Amnon, his elder brother. Absalom later usurped his father's throne, and the king had to run for his life. Furthermore, Absalom took his father's concubines and slept with them on the roof for all of Israel to see. The latter was God's judgment on David for sleeping with another man's wife, as outlined in 2 Samuel 12:11. Sleeping with another man's wife will always result in a curse.

"If my heart has been enticed by my neighbor's wife, or I have lurked at his door, then may my own wife grind grain for another, and may other men sleep with her. For that would be a heinous crime, an iniquity to be judged." Job 31:9-11 BSB

Men are gatekeepers of their families and bloodlines. This is why God set the man as the head of the house, and this is why you have your father's DNA. His transgressions or triumphs will filter to his wife, then to his children and to his grandchildren, to the third and fourth generations. When he commits adultery, he opens his bloodline to rape, sexual harassment, sexual abuse, sexual molestation, and oftentimes the women suffer more. As a result of his actions, his wife suffers a consequence that is not well known, recognized, or discussed. She is subject to subservience and adultery. This is based on the spiritual law of sowing and reaping.

A good friend of mine and a female minister of the gospel of Jesus Christ, confided about experiencing sudden and unwanted sexual attention and pursuit from a male co-worker. She was very surprised because although she and this co-worker were good friends, he never pursued her in such a manner. To her frustration, the pursuit of this co-worker became aggressive to the point of sexual harassment, and she fought aggressively to bring it to an end. This friend related that at the time of this occurrence, her marriage was in a challenging state. She confided that she later fell in love with and had an affair with a colleague —not the one who pursued her, but another —a course of action and a pattern of behavior that was unlike her personality. It was discovered later that her husband was cheating.

Adultery is the manifestation of a covenant-breaking spirit. Spirits transfer between partners. Men need to be cognizant of the fact that when they cheat, they open the door for their wives to cheat. Whether they have emotional affairs or go all the way into sexual sin, it's spiritual. The guilty husband opened the way for covenant-breaking spirits to be transferred, and to afflict and influence his wife. The law of sowing and reaping also takes effect. But that's not all; there's another consequence.

The Scripture from Job 31 mentioned above, says, *"then may my own wife grind grain for another."*

Let's examine the word "grind."

According to Dictionary.com, Grind means: to wear, smooth, or sharpen by abrasion or friction. To reduce to fine particles, as by pounding or crushing; bray, triturate, or pulverize. To perform the operation of reducing to fine particles. To rub harshly. Laborious, usually uninteresting work.[2]

Based on the Scripture and the meaning of the word "grind," a cheating husband, besides giving covenant-breaking spirits access to his wife, exposes her to be worn down and worn out by people and situations—especially in her place of work or professional life. It exposes her to be mishandled, abused and treated harshly to the point that she is reduced to a miniature or an unrecognizable version of herself. This includes spiritual, intellectual, psychological, and physical; wrong use, misuse, overuse, and abuse. He, by his behavior, opened the door which exposed his wife to working hard for others with very little reward or acknowledgement, and doing work that may not interest her, or for which she is overqualified. His wife may struggle to be promoted on her job or even struggle to obtain jobs that fit her qualifications. In three words, abused and reduced.

These are all consequences of not exercising control over his sexual desires. An adulterous husband will open doors in the spirit realm for demons to come flooding in. Women who have been in marriages where their husband cheated need to be aware of the consequences of their husband's actions and pray to break it - even if the couple has divorced. Those demons and consequences need to be forbidden from following the woman into the future, and into a new marriage.

Cheating may not always be the reality of a woman whose husband was unfaithful, but if it is, or was, to thine own self be true and deal with it in a direct manner. You don't have to confess your sins to everyone but confess it to someone who can bring deliverance, healing, and restoration to you. Demons dwell in secrets; they make it their stronghold. Furthermore, Proverbs 28:13 NKJV says, *"He who covers his sins will not prosper, But whoever confesses and forsakes them will have mercy."* I know of women who have cheated on their husbands then go home and pretend to be the lady of ladies, deceiving their husbands. I know of women who cheat on their husbands then invest time in highlighting and exposing other women who are unfaithful. It's deception and deflection at its finest. Women who behave like this do not prosper, and then they wonder why.

But, as I was saying, not all women necessarily cheat in return, but the transference of covenant-breaking spirits will happen, and the evidence of this will manifest in their marriage and in other areas of their life.

The traits of covenant-breaking spirits are; lying, scheming, deceiving, being double-faced, double-tongued, double-minded, envious, jealous, covetous, greedy, tale-bearing, gossiping, creating strife and dissension, being pretentious, playing the victim or being the villain, push and pull (where one time they love and want you around and another time they don't); witchy behaviors, manipulative, dominating, and intimidating.

These wives could begin to use witchcraft against their husbands or their lovers, or adapt behaviors associated with cognitive dissonance and schizophrenia. They may also adapt behaviors that indicate a break in agreement with themselves and life itself because their internal world has become destabilized and fragmented. As a result, some women become depressed, suicidal, and some begin cutting themselves. Some begin rejecting and hating themselves, and some develop low self-esteem or begin shaming and blaming themselves.

So that covenant breaking is fully understood, it is important to define covenant. A covenant, in its simplest expression, is an agreement between two parties. It means to bind oneself to another or come together in harmony. We can break covenant with others, and we can break covenant with ourselves.

Back to sexual sins of the father. Because of the father's sin of adultery, the pattern of being harassed sexually, abused, molested, or raped can remain in the bloodline and both females and males can be victimized. The same thing would happen if the father committed other sexual sins such as molestation, rape, or sexual perversion. When sexual sins are committed, the bloodline is opened to sexual sins being committed against those attached to the bloodline.

"For on account of a prostitute one is reduced to a piece of bread [to be eaten up], And the immoral woman hunts [with a hook] the precious life [of a man]." Proverbs 6:26 AMP

Not just sleeping with a prostitute, but adultery in general, will reduce a man's or a woman's life to a piece of bread. Women are not exempt from the consequences of committing adultery. Remember how King David had to be running for his life from his son Absalom in 2 Samuel 15:13-23? Committing adultery will open one's life to humiliation and being brought low.

Being anointed, or being used by God, does not exempt anyone from the consequences of their sin. David did not lose his kingship, nor his call, and the promised Messiah still came from his lineage. Nevertheless, he had to face the consequences of his sin; he was dethroned, and horribly humiliated —and by someone close to him—his son, Absalom.

Sexual sins have dire consequences, and when the devil entices us to sin he never shows us the humiliation written in fine print, only the glory and the glamor of the sin. Not only did David have to run for his life; amidst him running for his life, he was humiliated and cursed by a relative of the former King Saul. Sometimes when you are falling, you encounter nut jobs on the way down. There is always someone ready to make your life and what you are going through about them.

"When King David came to Bahurim, there came out a man of the family of the house of Saul, whose name was Shimei, the son of Gera, and as he came he cursed continually. And he threw stones at David and at all the servants of King David, and all the people and all the mighty men were on his right

hand and on his left. And Shimei said as he cursed, "Get out, get out, you man of blood, you worthless man! The Lord has avenged on you all the blood of the house of Saul, in whose place you have reigned, and the Lord has given the kingdom into the hand of your son Absalom. See, your evil is on you, for you are a man of blood."" 2 Samuel 16:5-8 ESV

Early Death and Aborted Destiny

Children would suffer aborted destinies or premature death if their parents had abortions or paid for them. In King David's situation, he had Uriah, Bathsheba's husband, killed. Consequently, Absalom and Amnon died prematurely. Tamar lived a life of desolation, as mentioned in 2 Samuel 13:20. Desolation means living a life of depression, sadness, emptiness, unfulfilled dreams, and unachieved goals.

Illegitimate Children

Illegitimate children—those born of adultery—also suffer because they were not covered adequately by their father since he was in an illegitimate relationship with their mother at the time of conception, which was the result of a broken covenant. Daughters of such fathers could experience not being covered and protected by male authority figures such as a husband, male spiritual leaders, and male authority figures in general.

Such women will find that they are preyed upon or sexually objectified by some male authority figures and their husbands will break covenant. Breaking covenant is not only restricted to committing adultery; there are examples listed earlier in this chapter. In addition to those mentioned, a husband breaking covenant could be demonstrated in a break in confidentiality in the marriage; he discusses things that should remain in the marriage with parents, siblings, family members, or friends instead of covering his wife at vulnerable times. It is also demonstrated in him putting his wife down behind her back or in her presence, lying about or misrepresenting her, downplaying her value or worth professionally, in his life, or in the lives of their children. Such a husband takes credit that should be given to her and is malicious towards her, even when there is no valid reason. Overall, he displays a lack of integrity. Such a husband will also take the side of her adversary in the time of trouble. Breaking covenant is exactly what it implies—a breach in harmony, synergy and agreement. Talking with other females about problems in the marriage is also breaking covenant. Unless that other woman is a therapist or someone giving professional assistance, it is breaking covenant. When covenant is broken, even secretly, the wife can feel the bond between her and her husband loosening.

Daughters born in illegitimate situations may have a history of having their heart broken by boyfriends and lovers. Also, they tend to be attracted to married men, or to men who are already in romantic relationships because that spirit of illegitimacy wants to remain in the bloodline. Males born in such situations will experience male authority figures in their lives behaving in a disloyal and dishonest manner. They will have to confront the covenant-breaking spirit to break such a pattern. It's the spirit that attracts or influences the behavior of such individuals.

The circumstances under which you came into this world is important, as it creates continuity of patterns, but it does not set destiny. Every child born into this world got here because God wanted that child to be here.

Psalm 139:13, 14 and Jeremiah 29:11 still apply to children born out of illegitimacy. God does not love them any less than those born within a marriage. However, the circumstances under which they were born creates challenges and struggles that children born legitimately may not have to face. Those challenges can be overcome by repenting for the sins of the parents and receiving deliverance to dislodge the demons. Nevertheless, it's always better to do things God's way.

Sexual immorality is glamorized and normalized now more than ever. The imagery that is being presented is that men are supposed to cheat, be unfaithful and have multiple sexual partners. Men are polygamous or polyamorous, they say. They are Alpha males, they say, but this is the work of the devil. This is a trick of the enemy to massage the ego of insecure and unhealed men who do not understand their role or function in their marriage, in the lives of their children, in their families, or in society. A male with a high sexual body count is an indication of a grown boy who never bothered to have the traumatized, broken, or abandoned little boy within him healed. He medicates pain with sex and masquerades behind the mask of being an Alpha male. A true Alpha male rules over his household and his desires well.

"A man without self-control is like a city broken into and left without walls." Proverbs 25:28 ESV

As a child, a man may not have had control over the things that were done to him - the abuse, abandonment, broken promises, or disappointments. But as an adult, he can take responsibility to address his childhood trauma instead of medicating it with sex, women, and romantic relationships. It's a mask, and most women can see it. While some women consider it a challenge to attempt to tame a womanizer, some women are turned off by men with a high sexual body count, since it reveals a man who lacks discretion, self-control, a man who is a serial cheater, a man who may be carrying or had been exposed to HIV or other sexually transmitted diseases (STDs), a man who most likely has a spiritual spouse, and a man who is in dire need of deliverance and therapy. But all is not lost.

"For this purpose the Son of God was manifested, that He might destroy the works of the devil." 1 John 3:8b KJV

Men need people in their lives who will be candid with them and hold them accountable for their harmful behaviors instead of enabling them. The devil makes it his goal to chase after men who have strong and significant destinies. The devil ensures that such men are traumatized early in their lives so that they never become the kings that God intended. Instead, they are ruled by sexual desires and lust.

The devil will always be the devil. He will always scheme against and deceive humans into getting themselves into bondages and negative cycles. But of course, he will sprinkle some glitter and spray some perfume on it to make it look attractive. God's standard of sexual purity and integrity remains the standard. God's Word has authority over social, cultural, and every other norm and pattern. Sexual immorality and adultery reduce a man's life to a piece of bread. A reduced man can never be an effective leader. When a man is reduced, a destiny is reduced, a family is reduced, and a bloodline is reduced. Also, according to Proverbs 6:29-35, he opens his life to the spirit of infirmity. It does not have to be a STD or HIV/AIDS; it could be any infirmity. The spirit of shame also attaches itself to him, and as a result, he will ever so often find himself in situations that brings him humiliation, embarrassment, or misfortune.

Men need intercessors and prayer warriors in their lives, whether it's their mother, sisters, or their wives. A man alone will abort, reduce, or struggle to fulfill his destiny if he does not have a praying woman in his life. A praying wife is a man's greatest asset.

All is Not Lost

Good things can come out of bad things. King David later married Bathsheba. King Solomon came from that union. God was clearly with Solomon, but he had an amplified version of his father's issues with women. Like David and Bathsheba, some marriages had its genesis in adultery. The reason for the adultery, where your walk with the Lord was at the time, is not in discussion. King David repented of his behavior; King David is not in hell.

I don't believe that you would go to hell if your marriage started in adultery, meaning that it's your second marriage and it started with you cheating on your former spouse. Both of you in the new marriage need to repent and move on with your lives; there is no need to live in condemnation. But in such situations, it is important to address the foundation of the union, which is adultery. Both parties need to repent, break agreements with spirits of adultery, sexual immorality, lust, deception, and covenant-breaking spirits. Apologize to your former spouse, if necessary. Also, I would recommend that both individuals go through deliverance. These actions will prevent those demons from infiltrating the bloodline.

WITCHCRAFT

"Thou shalt not suffer a witch to live." Exodus 22:18 KJV

Forbidden

Another way in which our ancestors brought curses upon us was their involvement in witchcraft. If our ancestors consulted witches, warlocks, sorcerers or approached anyone involved in occult activities to receive supernatural instructions, support, and assistance in any way, that person and their generation came under a curse. Witchcraft is evil; the Bible clearly condemns it. It's the dark side of spirituality.

"There shall not be found among you any one that maketh his son or his daughter to pass through the fire, or that useth divination, or an observer of times, or an enchanter, or a witch, or a charmer, or a consulter with familiar spirits, or a wizard, or a necromancer." Deuteronomy 18:10,11 KJV

When people approach the dark side for supernatural help and assistance, they don't see what happens in the background because Satan is a deceiver, and he works by stealth and secrecy. Neither he nor his agents will ever tell you what you are getting into when you consult spirits. The witch or wizard would never tell you that you are cursing your own life and bloodline by approaching them for help. For people who did this, in their mind, when they paid the money for whatever service they required, and once the service was received, the transaction was complete. On the contrary, it had just begun; a covenant was formed with darkness. The transaction with the human—whether a witch, wizard, or whatever they are called—is over. But the transaction with Satan and his demons has only just begun. The human was paid money or whatever was used as means of exchange. The demons do not need nor use money, but they expect to be paid; after all, they are the ones rendering the supernatural help. Their payment is cursing and afflicting that person and their bloodline. Satan, and by extension his demons' interaction with humans, will always be to steal, kill and destroy. Demons don't love humans. And although they present the impression that they are working on behalf of the human who engaged them, they are keeping that person in the bondage of perpetual negative cycles. Humans never win by approaching demons for assistance.

How It Works

Of course, that problem that was requested to be solved will be solved initially, partially, or permanently, depending on who the individual that the witchcraft was intended to affect. If the individual is a born-again believer and they are living an upright life as they should, then they are protected automatically by the blood of Jesus and God's holy angels. The demons will not be able to carry out any assignments against their life. However, the covenant between the individual who engaged darkness for supernatural assistance will still exist. Satan doesn't offer refunds. Even if the person whom witchcraft was used against stumbled and blundered along the way, if that person did not break covenant with God, God can still choose to protect that person supernaturally. There is a difference between falling into sin and breaking covenant with God. Falling into sin is missing the mark and falling short. That can happen to any believer in Christ, but breaking covenant is equivalent to backsliding and turning away from God. If the latter did not happen, God will protect His own and warn them so that they can pray against the assaults of darkness.

Secondly, if the individual that witchcraft was used against is surrounded by praying people, whether family or friends, the assignment of darkness can be intercepted and ended through the prayer and intercession of those people but the covenant between Satan and the individual who engaged darkness for supernatural help will still exist. I will mention once again, Satan doesn't offer refunds. Instead, he tricks humans into getting into covenant with him so that he can curse them and their bloodline.

In some cases, the situation that darkness was approached to be solved will be solved permanently. This could range from a promotion on a job, to a love potion, and everything else in between. That person will be allowed to feel as though they won and have the upper hand, but the role of any deceiver is to deceive. During time, other issues and challenges will arise in that person's life. When this happens, these individuals will not associate the other issues that arise—whether it's with their health, finances or with their children—to being cursed due to using witchcraft. These curses remain in the bloodline because these demons are attached to family members from generation to generation.

In some instances, these individuals tend to think that someone used witchcraft against them. This may result in them finding themselves in a perpetual cycle of using witchcraft for "protection." As a result, the devil and his demons gain access to establish themselves firmly within the bloodline of the family. Many generational issues such as sickness, poverty, challenges in marriages, divorce, abuse, and so on, are the result of ancestors approaching the dark side for help. Bloodline curses will only break when someone in the bloodline rises and breaks them.

Ignorance Does Not Mean Exemption

We are not always aware of what our ancestors did or in what way they rebelled against God, and Satan is legalistic; he does not care what you don't know. Satan does not care what you did not do, or if your parents or ancestors rebelled against God deliberately or out of ignorance. Once he has legal right to you, he will take it, use it, and even try to keep you in the dark by hiding the reason for your negative cycles from you. Rebelling against God gives Satan and his demons legal right to the bloodline. All is not lost; we can repent on their behalf.

I will say this to eliminate undue fear; if your sibling, or auntie or uncle, cousin or relative used or practice witchcraft, it will not affect you nor your children. Their sins only affect them and their children; it affects only those who came from their womb or loins. Therefore, you will not be cursed because of their sins, unless you participated.

Familiar

The word "familiar" is from the Latin "familiaris," meaning a "household servant."[3] Familiars are used by those who practice witchcraft. According to Merriam-Webster Dictionary, one of the meanings of witchcraft is: "Communication with the devil or with a familiar." These familiars are considered as a close friend or companion.

Familiars are supernatural or demonic entities that serve as guardians, protectors, and assist witches and diviners in performing their craft. Often, the familiars perform witchcraft and spells on behalf of the human companion. They could be summoned when magic needs to be performed, or they would use the person if the familiar possessed the human. Familiars can take on the form of a cat, often black; also, a dog, wolf, owl, and other types of birds. They could also take on the form of other animals such as horses, or objects such as a talisman or amulet. And finally, they can take the form of humans - although they may not always look quite human. Familiars do not appear as demons or ghosts; they appear realistic and natural in whatever form they take rather than looking ghostly or demonic. Sometimes they are kept in homes and treated like pets and fed a variety of things - from bread to blood. A familiar, regardless of what form they take, is basically a personal demon that often stays in the bloodline by extending itself to become the family demon. It usually initiates with one person. Although familiars are close companions to their humans, they are not always with them.

From the meaning of familiar, it's clear that familiars functioned as "household servants" or were used as a means of doing the "spiritual" or "supernatural" biddings of the family or individual. They are considered either malevolent, or "good" and "helpful." Witches, and those involved in witchcraft and divination, will have familiars. Besides having familiars, some witches even transform into objects such as broomsticks and other objects or household pets such as black cats or birds to access places unnoticeably.

Witchcraft is on the increase. Believers in Christ cannot be ignorant of the enemy's devices. More and more we will see open confrontations between the true sons of God and practitioners of witchcraft as in the days of Elijah when he confronted the prophets of Jezebel and as in the days of Moses when he confronted Pharaoh about freeing God's people.

"Then the LORD said to Moses and Aaron, When Pharaoh says to you, 'Prove yourselves by working a miracle,' then you shall say to Aaron, 'Take your staff and cast it down before Pharaoh, that it may become a serpent.'" So Moses and Aaron went to Pharaoh and did just as the LORD commanded. Aaron cast down his staff before Pharaoh and his servants, and it became a serpent. Then Pharaoh summoned the wise men and the sorcerers, and they, the magicians of Egypt, also did the same by their secret arts. For each man cast down his staff, and they became serpents. But Aaron's staff swallowed up their staffs." Exodus 7:8-12 ESV

Love Potions

Witches use familiars when they perform magic for love spells and love potions. The demon assigned to that spell or potion performs the task of creating a bond between the targeted "lover" and the person who used the potion or spell to obtain a desired lover. Such relationships are obviously not genuine since the individuals are bonded demonically. This is why some romantic relationships don't make sense. When a male who in times past was not interested or seriously interested in a female romantically is suddenly "madly in love" or is obsessed with that female, it's possible that magic was involved. It's now a trend for women to turn to witchcraft to obtain a desired romantic partner.

Fetishes

A thing can have a familiar spirit. Witches and those who practices witchcraft use fetishes. A fetish is a dwelling place of a demon or entity. The word fetish being used in relation to a sexual desire and the gratification thereof was a definition that was added later, but initially it was meant to describe an object inhabited by a demon. When someone wants to exercise control over another person romantically, professionally or otherwise, they go to a witch to get a fetish and then give it to the person. A fetish can be clothes, jewelry, ornaments, and the like. It is important, especially for males, to be discerning when accepting gifts from females. Always keep a smile and a "No, thank you" handy. Saying no could save you a lot of trouble. Some women are cunning but can masquerade as innocent or pretend to be pure in intention.

Alter Egos

Witches and those who perform witchcraft and divination are not the only individuals who keep familiars; regular people can have familiars too. In such instances, the familiar is a demon spirit. It takes on the form of an alter ego but serves the same purpose of aiding, assisting, or enhancing the person's skills, abilities, toxicity, or simply influencing their daily choices and decisions. In such instances, the familiar possesses the individual rather than being an external companion. I've heard someone fondly refer to the familiar that possess them as their "other person." There are famous celebrities who claim to have alter egos; some have claimed to have several. Psychopaths, sociopaths, and narcissists tend to have alter egos.

They Gather Information

Familiars, regardless of what form they take, can be sent to gather information on behalf of their human. I've counseled women who were (or still) married to a narcissist, and these women were always confused about how the narcissist knew exactly what they are doing although they were separated or divorced. The narcissist's familiar gave them information; that's how they knew.

Spiritual Inheritance

Familiar spirits create the Hydra cycle. Whether they pretend to be good or "malevolent," familiar spirits always want to remain with their human companion and remain in their bloodline. They initiate contact with their human companion in times of distress such as illness, times of grief, or if the individual is struggling to survive – for example, they lost income. The familiar shows up to give a way out by offering the human supernatural powers. I had an experience in which familiars showed up to offer me a way out. I was struggling financially at the time because I was unemployed. They were persistent. I had to keep pushing back. I was not about to break covenant with God because of difficult times. Tough times don't last, tough people do. I was saved at eleven years old. I never had that type of interaction with the dark side before, and I was not about to begin just because I was going through a difficult time. It was in that moment that I made the decision that if the God whom I serve could not take me out of the situation, then I was not going to be out. God showed up as expected, not when I wanted Him to but when He chose to show up. Nevertheless, it was on time.

A familiar could be inherited, meaning it's passed down from one person to the other in the family at the death of its human companion. This passing down usually happens from parent to child. A familiar could also be gifted to a human by a spirit spouse, and sometimes it takes on the form of a spirit child.

A spirit spouse can be considered a familiar because it's connected to a particular individual or family. A spirit spouse can remain in the bloodline and move from parent to child throughout the generations until it is divorced, and the agreement is broken. The same can happen with spirits of idolatry, spirits of pride, spirits of rejection, the spirit of divorce, spirits of poverty, spirits of infirmity, spirits associated with early death, covenant-breaking spirits that lead to cheating, spirits of witchcraft, the spirit of Jezebel, and the like.

Blind Practitioners

Let say an ancestor was openly a witch or warlock, but the following generations distanced themselves from that practice but did not break the agreement, covenant, or disassociate themselves from the altar of their parent or grandparent; that spirit of witchcraft remains in the bloodline. This is why some people are blind witches. A blind witch is someone who does not know that they are a witch, but they are one because the spirit of witchcraft is a part of their spiritual inheritance. Witchcraft is their spiritual inheritance, so these individuals tend to be manipulative, controlling and Jezebelic, or in times of crises they default to witchy tactics. This happens even if they are saved; this is why going through deliverance after salvation is important. Salvation is one thing; deliverance is another. Every believer in Christ needs to receive the ministry of deliverance. You cannot be a sinner all your life, become a believer in Jesus and then think that the demons will leave automatically. Some do leave at salvation, while others need to be addressed directly and cast out, especially the ones that were inherited. Inherited demons are stubborn. They see the individual as property, so they need to be addressed deliberately.

Based on Galatians 5:19-21, witchcraft is a manifestation of the work of the flesh. This means that witchcraft originates from the fleshly or carnal nature of people. At its core, witchcraft is wanting to exercise unauthorized control over other people or over situations. It will begin as being habitually manipulative, domineering, or intimidating. People who are like this will lie, scheme, deceive, or play the victim or the villain. They create strife and chaos, whether it's among family members, friends, or co-workers. If these tactics fail, then such individuals oftentimes turn to supernatural means by consulting a witch or warlock, or even practicing witchcraft on their own. Their goal is to get the upper hand in the situation by any means necessary.

Witchcraft in Today's Culture

Popular ways to practice witchcraft in our times are not always intended to cause harm. Although the motivation is not evil, it is still witchcraft because it was not authorized by God. Humans attempting to control and initiate engagement and interaction with the spirit realm outside of God is witchcraft, whether it is considered harmless or not. We were never authorized by God to carve out or create our own path to spirituality or spiritual enlightenment. When humans reach out to the spirit realm outside of the Most High God, they will receive engagement and response from that realm, but those engagements will be from evil spirits masquerading as good and helpful until they are ready to show themselves in their true form.

Humans are spirit beings; we have a soul, and we live in a body, which is the house of the spirit. At the core, we are spirit, not body or soul. Because of this, there is a natural desire to want to connect with something spiritual or supernatural. Outside of a genuine relationship with Christ, humans will seek some other form of spirituality, unfortunately to their detriment. Seeking spiritual connection outside of Christ will lead to destruction. And unfortunately, such connections don't come with warning labels. These practices are not new.

"That which has been is that which will be [again], And that which has been done is that which will be done again. So there is nothing new under the sun." Ecclesiastes 1:9 AMP

Forms of Witchcraft used by non-Christians and Many Who Profess to be Christians

- Opening of the third eye

- Use of healing stones and crystals

- Use of sound bowls

- Psychic readings

- Use of Ouija Boards

- Practicing astrology

- Use of acupuncture

- Practicing hypnotism

- Using tarot cards

- Practicing kundalini

- Reading chakras

- Practicing yoga

- Use of horoscopes

- Partaking in Halloween

- Use of spirit guides

- Reincarnation beliefs

- Practicing feng shui

- Use of dream catchers

- Superstitious beliefs and practices

- Use of fortune cookies

- Palm reading

- Use of rosary beads

- Belief in numerology

- Smudging: Burning sage, Burning of Palo Santo

- Gemstones

- Divination

- Law of attraction

- Tea leaf reading

- Angel worship

- Praying to statutes of deities

- Use of sex magic

- Nature worship

- Goddess worship

- Heightened senses of spiritual awareness

- Other New age beliefs not mentioned

- Dream manipulation – manipulate self-into other people's dreams

- Practicing astral projection

- Love spells

This list is in no way exhaustive. Thou shalt not suffer a witch to live as stated in Exodus 22:18 KJV is a law of God. The law of God is spiritual, and humans are spiritual. Hence, practicing witchcraft brings the practitioner under the curse of death. When someone who practiced witchcraft becomes a believer in Jesus Christ, that individual needs to break agreement with the spirit of death.

Hydra Runs on These Spiritual Laws

Shall the prey be taken from the mighty, or the lawful captive delivered?
Isaiah 49:24 KJV

Sympathetic Magic

Sympathetic magic, also known as the law of contact, states that things that have been in contact with each other will continue to act on each other at a distance after the physical contact has been broken.[4] The law of contact is effective because life is spiritual. We are human, but at the core we are spiritual beings, and as a result, spiritual laws and principles apply to and affect us all. The law of contact is a spiritual principle. The law of contact works between people and people, people and places, people and things, and people and experiences.

People and People

Sympathetic magic is why two people could end a relationship and one or both parties still communicate or try to remain in contact after the relationship has ended. Some people even cyber stalk their exes. It's also why former romantic partners can reignite a relationship easily after many months or years apart.

People and Places

Let's say that you were at a party where there was glitter, smoking and the like; when you leave to go home you will have glitter on your clothes and body, and the smell of whatever was being smoked will be imbedded in your clothes, skin, and hair. By leaving the event to return home, you did not get rid of the contaminants from you automatically. Even after you've had a shower to remove the smell and glitter, the experience is lodged in your subconscious mind as a memory - the sounds, sights, smells, and other details of that experience. Depending on the experience, you may have decided that you want to continue having experiences like that, or you may not want to have another experience like that.

It's the same with the law of contact. Things that have been in contact with each other will continue to act on each other at a distance after the physical contact has been broken.

People and Experiences

The law of contact could exist between an individual and a toxic family, a toxic church, or a toxic workplace. Although someone may have exited an environment, a bond could remain subconsciously between the two, which could result in them using that same situation or environment that they were so eager to exit in times past as a standard to measure every new environment, situation, or person. Like Lot's wife, instead of appreciating, engaging completely, and adjusting to what is happening in their lives now, they keep looking back at the past, although God brought them out.

On the other hand, some people will remember the toxic experiences and those attached to it with resentment and bitterness. This is still the law of contact exercising authority in that individual's life.

If God moved you out of a toxic situation but you are looking back constantly to see if God has judged or punished those connected for what they did to you - or if something bad happened to one of those individuals and you attribute it to God judging them for what they did to you, then the demons connected to those experiences are still exercising authority over you through the law of contact.

God judges people and He vindicates His own but obsessing over others being judged and you being vindicated is a sign that you are still bound to that situation. The law of contact is still exercising authority over you. When God brings you out, get all the way out. Allow God to decide how and when He will handle oppressors and those who caused you harm.

"What shall we say then? Is there injustice on God's part? By no means! For he says to Moses, "I will have mercy on whom I have mercy, and I will have compassion on whom I have compassion." So then it depends not on human will or exertion, but on God, who has mercy." Romans 9:14-16 ESV

Sympathetic Magic Programs Personality

Sympathetic magic creates lags and delays in someone adjusting and adapting effectively to anything new as it keeps alive a craving for the old thing, even if the old thing was toxic and caused trauma. Time and distance may cause them to forget the intensity of the pain that the toxic environments caused them. Hence, they only remember the good things of past situations. Sympathetic magic programs their personality too. For example, if someone was in a relationship where there were constant conflicts, fights and quarrels, when they enter a new relationship, (although that new individual is gentler and more peaceful) the partner who is used to conflicts may stir up fights and quarrels in their new relationship because an appetite exists for strife and conflict.

Some males expect their spouse to engage them sexually like someone in their past because sympathetic magic keeps them tied to those experiences. Hence, during times of intimacy, instead of engaging with the person in his presence, he retrieves memories of sexual encounters with an ex and tries to recreate those experiences. As a result, his spouse is now expected to behave sexually like his ex. She is now presented with the unpleasant experience of conflicting with her spouse's past sexual experiences and encounters. She may even have to raise this as a conversation so that he becomes conscious of the fact that he needs to adapt and adjust sexually to the person in his presence. This type of behavior has been the reality for far too many women. It's not only sloppy but it is unfair as well. It is always the responsibility of the individual involved to adapt and adjust to the new situation in every way. No one walks around wearing winter clothes during summer. People adapt to season changes automatically. This type of versatility needs to be brought into every area of our lives.

Unhealed Trauma

Through constant harassment that leads to trauma, demons that possess toxic people create a bond with the individual that's being traumatized. It is through these bonds that the demon that controls the abuser is transferred to the abused. This is why hurt people may hurt other people and traumatized people can traumatize other people. This is why people in abusive or toxic work situations may go home and be abusive or toxic to their families. I said "may" because some people are able to transition psychologically as they commute between work and home so that they don't take the residue of that negative environment home. Others are unable to do this. The decision to transition must be deliberate.

The abuse could happen the opposite way, where someone who is being abused at home, or who grew up in an abusive home environment, may be abusive to their co-workers or subordinates. When an abused individual remains unhealed and undelivered, they become abusers when they obtain power. Abusive adults tend to have unhealed childhood trauma.

Based on everything I mentioned regarding the law of contact, it's clear that this law paves the way for soul ties and the transference of spirits. This type of transference of spirits is evident in women who had toxic Jezebelic mothers-in-law and they in turn become toxic and Jezebelic to the wives of their sons.

While the abused was being abused, they lost power, oftentimes due to no fault of their own - but the moment they gained power in a situation, whether at work or at home, they became a conduit for the abuse that they experienced. You will always see the true nature and place of trauma in a person when they are given power and authority over people or situations.

Unhealed trauma is also why someone can see you and dislike you instantly, as you remind them of someone who caused them trauma or heartbreak. Because of the soul tie that still exists between them and the person who caused them pain, you suffer resentment, rejection and even abuse at their hand. A demon that possesses a toxic person can also try to form a soul tie with you by harassing and abusing you constantly through the possessed.

If the demon can bring you to a place where you hate or resent the individual, it has formed a soul tie with you successfully. Spirits are transferred through soul ties or the law of contact which states that things that have been in contact with each other continue to act on each other at a distance after the physical contact has been broken. (Wikipedia) I've seen someone sit under an abusive superior, and although this individual suffered at their hand and constantly complained about this superior, they behaved exactly like that superior after that superior left that working situation.

I would like to remind us that possessed people don't all act crazy or appear as if something is wrong with them. Some are unusually prideful, arrogant, vindictive, and the like. Abusers tend to be psychopathic, sociopathic, narcissistic, obsessed, or controllers. All are toxic. Toxic personalities can break you down psychologically, physically, and spiritually, and even cause death. The best strategy is to avoid them.

The devil works in many ways to keep our lives in negative cycles. The enemy uses both our bloodline and the environment that we interact with daily - whether it's work, church, or social settings. Always remember that in the same way that the toxins in the souls of others can infect you without you noticing it consciously, you can do the same to others if you don't make deliberate attempts to detox and halt the transference of spirits. Hydra has several heads, and sympathetic magic or the law of contact are powerful conduits of the enemy for the transference of spirits and continuation of negative reoccurrences.

Whenever God brings us out of a toxic family situation, working environment, or church environment, we need to bind sympathetic magic and break the power of the law of contact or the soul ties with these toxic and negative experiences and individuals so that we can move on freely. You need to forgive such individuals and situations and pray that the blood of Jesus forms a protective barrier between you and them so that their associated demons are not transferred to you.

Divorce

Research shows that people who had been divorced once have a higher probability of being divorced again if they remarry, and this possibility increases even greater with a third marriage. Statistics are an important source of information about patterns and trends. Statistics, however, are not personal prophecy. Therefore, it's not necessary to come into agreement with it on a personal level. Someone could acknowledge the statistics but decide that they will not be a statistic. Again, we see Hydra at work riding on the law of contact - in this case, contact with the spirit of divorce and other covenant-breaking spirits.

As a result, divorced people need to break agreement with the spirit of divorce and every other covenant-breaking spirit. Even if situations which led to the divorce were not the individual's fault, this is no reason to neglect the covenant-breaking spirits connected to the spirit of divorce. Maybe a partner cheated, or broke covenant in some other way that led to the divorce, or he or she may have even been abusive. Spousal abuse, whether physical, psychological, financial, or spiritual, is still a manifestation of a covenant-breaking spirit. When two individuals marry, neither party stood at the altar and made an agreement to abuse the other; they made an agreement to love and cherish each other. Abuse in any form is the manifestation of a covenant-breaking spirit.

Two individuals become one flesh through marriage. In the same way that STDs can be transferred from the unfaithful partner to the faithful partner, the covenant-breaking partner's spirits will be transferred to the faithful partner, including covenant-breaking spirits. This is true especially if situations leading to the divorce, or the divorce itself, were difficult and traumatic. This is why people who were in such situations refuse to remarry or have a low tolerance for challenges in the next relationship, or they become jaded. This status of being jaded can mask itself as "wisdom," but that's not always the case. Often, at the core of this status lies the residue of the trauma from the situations that led to divorce and the divorce process itself, especially if it was difficult. Hence the reason I encourage deliverance and counseling after divorce.

Oaths, Altars, and Agreements

Deliverance is needed to be free from the oaths, altars, covenants, and agreements that our ancestors made. Although we may have never known or even met these individuals, because of the law of contact, we are tied to them until we sever the tie with the name or the blood of Jesus Christ. I will never forget the day when a familiar spirit from my bloodline showed up in my dream to accuse me of not keeping my promise. I was totally surprised, as I never once engaged or had an agreement with darkness. Yet, I was being accused of not keeping my promise. Someone in my bloodline made an agreement for which I was being held responsible. Families are like the body of Christ; although they are many members, all are one. When a family name enters into an agreement with darkness, the familiar spirit does not care which individual did or did not make an agreement with them; they hold the entire bloodline responsible to keep the covenant.

Items

The law of contact transcends beyond people and situations; it affects items too. I used to dispose of my hair that broke off while combing in the garbage; I don't anymore. A former Christian hairdresser of mine tried to use my hair to perform witchcraft against me. Be careful who has access to your hair. If you feel uncomfortable or uneasy about a hairdresser, regardless of how good they are, move on. Make your spiritual and overall wellbeing your priority, not hairstyles and trends. Because of my experience, I am the only one who handles my hair. It's not that I will never have anyone handle my hair again. Perhaps I will, when I find someone that the spirit of God in me trusts.

Whatever was done to an object will affect the person that was in contact with that object, whether it was a part of their body, such as hair, fingernails, or such. This is not to make you paranoid but pay attention when items of clothing or personal possessions are missing, especially when you are amid hateful or jealous people. People will steal things that belong to you or items that you were in contact with to do witchcraft against you. Jealousy has a spirit of death assigned to it. Song of Solomon 8:6b KJV says, *"Jealousy is cruel as the grave."* Someone with a jealous spirit will eliminate you because they are influenced by a spirit of death. People have conspired against me and used witchcraft against me because they were jealous of a relationship that I had. A friend will betray a friend because of jealousy. Ignoring a jealous person in your close circle is like cuddling a snake. At some point it will bite you or try to swallow you whole.

The Law of Similarity

This law states that like things will produce like things.[6] A toxic parent will produce a toxic child or children. A toxic older generation will produce a toxic younger generation. Traumatized people tend to traumatize other people. Hurt people will hurt other people. Unbroken negative spiritual inheritances will continue as a pattern in the bloodline. We cannot escape our origins unless God intervenes, neither can we produce a healthy lineage unless God heals us. Spiritual issues cannot be solved by our might or power, but by the spirit of the Lord (Zechariah 4:6).

The Law of Similarity also states that an effect resembles a cause. When soul ties are unbroken, people will be attracted to or will attract what hurt them in the past, whether it's an individual or an environment. This is why some people can move from one toxic church or leader to another, or from one toxic work situation to another. Moving out of the environment or situation is not enough; the law of similarity needs to be nullified so that the spirits that oppressed you in the previous situation do not continue onward with you.

The law of similarity expresses itself strongly in unbroken soul ties. Unbroken soul ties are why individuals, especially women, end up in cycles of toxic relationships. They keep attracting the same type of men. This is also why some men like a certain type of woman, or vice versa. This reflects a soul tied to a "type" of romantic partner. They are soul-tied to a familiar spirit, which was the type of spirit that was in the person who caused them pleasure or pain initially.

Soul ties are stronger through painful situations that resulted in trauma. Through the trauma of an abusive or traumatic relationship, the demon that possessed the abuser initiated a bond with the abused. As a result, they expect their new romantic partner to look, feel and function like their ex although their ex made their lives hellish. Unknown to them, demons travel through the law of similarity to continue their work of harassing an individual. Unbroken, unhealthy soul ties are conduits for the Hydra.

Familiar spirits live in trauma and hurt. Therefore, not only breaking the law of similarity, but forgiveness is key in such situations. Unforgiveness does not harm the person that's unforgiven; it only harms the person who refuses to forgive. Forgiveness does not always result in restoration of the relationship; it simply means letting go of offenses. Some say that to forgive is divine. Once you are born again, you have the capacity to forgive, because you have God's divine nature.

"By which he has granted to us his precious and very great promises, so that through them you may become partakers of the divine nature, having escaped from the corruption that is in the world because of sinful desire." 2 Peter 1:4 ESV

Rachel and Her Daddy's Gods

"...Nor sit in the seat of scoffers!" Psalm 1:1 NASB

"Now Laban had gone to shear his sheep, and Rachel had stolen the household idols that were her father's. And Jacob stole away, unknown to Laban the Syrian, in that he did not tell him that he intended to flee. So he fled with all that he had. He arose and crossed the river, and headed toward the mountains of Gilead. And Laban was told on the third day that Jacob had fled. Then he took his brethren with him and pursued him for seven days' journey, and he overtook him in the mountains of Gilead. But God had come to Laban the Syrian in a dream by night, and said to him, "Be careful that you speak to Jacob neither good nor bad."

So Laban overtook Jacob. Now Jacob had pitched his tent in the mountains, and Laban with his brethren pitched in the mountains of Gilead. And Laban said to Jacob: "What have you done, that you have stolen away unknown to me, and carried away my daughters like captives taken with the sword? Why did you flee away secretly, and steal away from me, and not tell me; for

I might have sent you away with joy and songs, with timbrel and harp? And you did not allow me to kiss my sons and my daughters. Now you have done foolishly in so doing. It is in my power to do you harm, but the God of your father spoke to me last night, saying, 'Be careful that you speak to Jacob neither good nor bad.' **And now you have surely gone because you greatly long for your father's house, but why did you steal my gods?"**

Then Jacob answered and said to Laban, "Because I was afraid, for I said, 'Perhaps you would take your daughters from me by force.' **With whomever you find your gods, do not let him live. In the presence of our brethren, identify what I have of yours and take it with you." For Jacob did not know that Rachel had stolen them.**

And Laban went into Jacob's tent, into Leah's tent, and into the two maids' tents, but he did not find them. **Then he went out of Leah's tent and entered Rachel's tent. Now Rachel had taken the household idols, put them in the camel's saddle, and sat on them. And Laban searched all about the tent but did not find them. And she said to her father, "Let it not displease my lord that I cannot rise before you, for the manner of women is with me." And he searched but did not find the household idols."**

Genesis 31:19-35 NKJV **(Emphasis mine)**

Rachel was Jacob's favorite wife. She was the woman that he wanted, but because of the rules of the culture that he was in, he had to marry her older sister Leah first. He did not love Leah. At this point in their lives, narrated in the portion of Scripture above, Jacob was taking his wives and children and was returning to his country and his father's house. Laban,

Rachel's father, was clearly an idol worshipper. Hence, she was used to worshipping idols. Jacob, her husband, on the other hand, came from a lineage of worshipping the true God. He was the grandson of Abraham.

Rachel is a picture of plurality in worship. Her marriage to Jacob aligned her with his God and the God of his fathers, Abraham and Isaac, the true and living God - but she still wanted to remain in covenant with the gods that she knew from childhood. They were familiar to her. In Rachel's situation, she did not have a familiar such as a demonic pet or person, as was discussed in the previous chapter. Instead, her bloodline had a spirit or spirits which were familiar to it. The spirits were connected to idol worship. Idols are habitations for demonic entities or familiars. The demons of her father's idols were familiar to Rachel and the bloodline in general. Any demonic entity that has attached itself to a bloodline is a familiar spirit to that bloodline. Familiar spirits come in two ways: as a familiar, as discussed in the previous chapter, or as it was with Rachel. Most people fall into the latter category. Demons attach themselves to the bloodline one way or the other; through oaths, altars, agreements, and idolatry.

Idolatry

Familiar spirits are attached to the bloodline and can range from the spirit of poverty, to pride, and everything in between. A familiar spirit can be identified easily by its primary traits. How does it behave? What is it doing? It's very simple to identify. Although the type of familiar spirits could vary from family to family, if it is attached to the bloodline, it's a familiar spirit, or a family spirit to that household or lineage.

Functioning through the law of contact, familiar spirits like to form soul ties with people often on a subliminal level. It causes its victims to become attached to it through people, places, things, or traditions. This is what happened to Rachel as she was attached to objects, the idols of her father. An idol can be a person, place, thing, or image. In her case, these idols were images and were also referred to as Teraphim. Teraphim were human figures of various sizes. Some were small, about the size of figurines, two to three inches in length, while others were large. These teraphim were made of wood, clay, and precious stones. Most of the teraphim were images of female deities, but some represented male deities and others were made to resemble ancestors. These idols were revered as bringers of fertility, prosperity, and good health.[7]

The Bible never mentioned why Rachel stole her father's gods, but now that we understand the law of contact, we understand that Rachel was most likely soul-tied to her daddy's gods. And now that we understand similarity, we know that like things will produce like things. Idol worshippers will produce idol worshippers.

In addition to that, Rachel was barren for a while, while Leah, on the other hand, was birthing a lot of babies. Perhaps Rachel wanted the gods as fertility charms. But in her culture, the household gods were inherited by the sons at their father's death, or they were handed over when a son reached the patriarchal age. Daughters did not inherit the gods. The son holding the family gods was entitled to his father's properties. This could have been why Laban was so adamant about getting the gods back, as he wanted to secure his son's inheritance and succession, but Rachel had already bonded with the family demon.

Michal and her Teraphim

Michal, King Saul's daughter and David's wife, may have pulled a similar feat of stealing a teraphim, but hers seemed to have been human size. She used her teraphim to trick her father regarding her husband's presence while he escaped her father's sword.

"And Michal took the household idol and laid it on the bed, put a pillow of goats' hair at its head, and covered it with clothes. And when Saul sent messengers to take David, she said, "He is sick". Then Saul sent the messengers [again] to see David, saying, "Bring him up to me on his bed [if necessary], so that I may kill him. When the messengers came in, there was the household idol on the bed with a quilt of goats' hair at its head. Saul said to Michal, "Why have you deceived me like this and let my enemy go, so that he has escaped?" Michal answered Saul, "He said to me, 'Let me go! Why should I kill you?'" 1 Samuel 19:13-17 AMP

It is interesting that a human-sized household idol was in David's house. Perhaps Michal had it hidden from him in the same way that Rachel failed to mention to her husband that she stole her daddy's idols. Both Rachel and Michal were soul-tied to the idols of their fathers. The demons attached to those idols formed a soul tie with the people who worshipped them; in this case it was Rachel and Michal. Rachel's sister Leah seemed to not care much about those gods, as Leah was never mentioned in relation to them. For the curse on the bloodline to continue, the demons need to find someone in the next generation to become familiar and comfortable with them. There has to be agreement. Rachel and Michal came into agreement with them to the point that they stole them.

Idolatry is one of the simplest ways for familiar spirits to establish themselves in a family. Idolatry is not restricted to worshipping fallen deities; an idol could be any person, place or thing that we esteem higher than Christ Jesus.

Sometimes an idol could be a lover; you love that person more than you love God. They consume all of your waking hours, your energy, and resources. If you are willing to rebel against God to win or keep that person, then they are an idol. God is jealous. He does not want us loving anyone more than we love Him. He is not just jealous; His name is Jealous. *"(for you shall worship no other god, for the Lord, whose name is Jealous, is a jealous God)"* Exodus 34:14 NKJV. We are not to make the Lord jealous with any relationship in our lives, be it idols, lovers, children, or friendships. Put no one before Him.

Seated

Rachel sat on her father's idols. Sitting is an important posture in the natural and spiritual realm. For example, a king sits on his throne to rule. In government, Parliament or the Senate/House of Representatives must be seated to make decisions, rules and laws. The Bible tells us that we are seated in heavenly places with Christ (Ephesians 2:6). Where someone is seated when ruling is the basis of their authority. Rachel ruled from being seated on her father's gods. It was not a one-time incident; it was her heart's posture revealed in a one-time incident.

"Blessed is the man who walks not in the counsel of the wicked, nor stands in the way of sinners, nor sits in the seat of scoffers." Psalm 1:1 ESV

To scoff is to show contempt by insulting words and actions. This implies a prideful disposition. Prideful people always lift themselves up above others. Wherever there is pride there will be witchcraft. In Galatians 5:19-21 NIV, witchcraft is listed as a work of the flesh. It comes from the soulish realm and displays itself in people through the need to control situations and other people, by natural or supernatural means.

Although Jacob clearly loved Rachel, this does not mean that she did not manipulate, dominate, or control situations to have her way. Following up on the meaning of familiar, people who use familiar spirits of any form are seeking to control the situation; such individuals use this measure to keep or turn things in their favor. They use the familiar spirit to "serve" them.

Also, this could have impacted how she interacted with her sister Leah and Leah's children. Leah was Jacob's first wife. That may have created the basis for Leah's sons hating and resenting Rachel's only son and their youngest brother at the time, Joseph. Talk about family drama. Some truths are uncomfortable. I know we like to see "good" Bible characters as all bright and shiny, but they were flawed like every other human.

Based on the Scripture above, there is a blessing for not sitting in the seat of scoffers. That lets us know that if you are sitting in the seat of a scoffer, you are under a curse. Someone is either blessed or cursed; there is no neutral zone. So, those who sit on their household gods take on the posture of a scoffer, and they are under a curse. Scoffers would sit on their family gods and lie, make excuses, and pretend to be walking in freedom when they are not. Sometimes they want to serve God genuinely, but since they never handled the family demons, they lurk, waiting, even years later, to reel them in.

No one steals anything by accident. Rachel did not take those gods accidentally; it was a strategic decision. We need to be careful what we "take" from our father's house. We could be opening the door for Hydra to remain. We cannot worship the true and living God while being soul-tied and in covenant with family demons, whether deliberately, or subliminally. The fact that she stole the gods indicated that her husband was not involved in her worship of idols. She brought them along secretly and remained in agreement with gods that her husband did not worship. By her actions, she broke agreement with her husband to remain connected to familiar spirits. Although Rachel was her husband's favorite wife, she struggled with barrenness. Her sister Leah did not have this issue. Rachel died earlier than her sister. Remember - Jacob pronounced death on anyone found with the idols! She was not found with the idols by her father, but the demons knew that she had them.

Do you see the negative effect of her actions? It's important that you examine your life to identify the areas where you are still sitting on family idols, and then repent and fall out of agreement with those demons and mindsets. Demons don't serve humans; it's a deception from demons to keep humans in bondage. They serve Satan.

Besides, many in the church today are like Rachel; they want to serve God but bring along their familiar household gods – gods that they've known all their lives, to which they are soul-tied. In His sovereignty, God was removing Rachel from an idolatrous culture, but the idolatrous culture remained inside of her.

Some people refuse to break covenant with their father's house and the gods of their father's house. They idolize the way that they were raised, although it was not the best. They are simply stuck in the past, and such individuals will ever so often reference the way they were raised and even consciously and unconsciously try to replicate those behaviors that they experienced as children in their own household as adults. Sometimes their idolization is their way of compensating for unhealed woundedness, trauma, or disappointment that they experienced in that childhood space. This idolization exists because of the soul ties that exists between the individual and the family demon. Many are bound in this way but are too blinded and bound by pride to see it or even acknowledge it. The spirit of pride is another demon that compensates for unhealed woundedness, trauma, and rejection. This is the sole reason why people hold on to familiar spirits. It is a common connector.

No one grew up in a perfect home; anyone who tries to project this image is under a strong delusion. There are good things about the way that we were raised that we want to hold on to, and there are things that we absolutely need to reject. What we should never do is steal the idols from our father's house. The idols that our fathers worshipped is what caused their houses to fail. If we steal their idols, we will continue their cycle of failing. Although he used so many ways to trick her husband, Jacob, Rachel's father's house failed. On every occasion he failed. God prospered her husband, and as a result, he left with the wealth of Laban's house. God gave it to him.

HYDRA: A RULING SPIRIT

"Forgetting what is behind and straining toward what is ahead..."
Philippians 3:13b NIV

We've already established that Hydra is a marine spirit. Marine spirits function from the marine kingdom. The marine kingdom is beneath the sea. The world's ocean is vast and largely unexplored. There is an entire kingdom beneath the water. Disney did not dream up the idea of the mermaid. Marvel did not dream up the idea of the fish man. Some things do exist hidden from our view, and what we don't know can harm us. The marine kingdom majors in mind control. Mind control is soul control. Because of this, the Hydra, which is a ruling spirit, as well as other familiar spirits, can control and influence how a person or group of people think, feel, and choose.

A ruling spirit always has other spirits under its control. Based on the myth of the Hydra, it had anywhere between two to nine heads. Heads always represent authority or rule. Because of its posture as a ruling spirit, the Hydra can keep not only families, but places, and people groups under the influence of different demons. With the Hydra's level of power, the people and places can be trapped in different demonic cycles.

Place

A familiar spirit can also exist in a place, such as within an organization, a company, a region, or within a territory or nation. This is why you may see everyone in a certain place behave the same, have the same propensity, weakness, or challenge. Whenever an outsider comes into that space, they can fall under the influence of that spirit if they don't discern and resist it. This is also why someone you know may develop behaviors like someone they associate with from a certain place that has a certain stronghold.

The person may not be a part of that environment, but by association with someone from it, the familiar spirit that is attached to their associate becomes familiar to them too. Someone who did not behave in a certain way in times past, changed as soon as they moved to a new place. That's because they came under the influence of the ruling spirit of that environment. When we want to bring such individuals into freedom, we must first address and break the power and influences of the ruling spirit. The ruling spirit can be identified easily by what is happening. What is the prevailing issue in that environment? Whatever it is, that's the name of the ruling spirit. If everyone is poor or struggling financially, then the ruling spirit is poverty. If people in the environment are sexually immoral, then the ruling spirit is sexual immorality. If people tend to fall ill, then the ruling spirit is the spirit of infirmity. Before such individuals can be freed, the mind control exercised by the ruling spirit must be broken.

Nation

There are some nationalities that are extremely narcissistic. It's more likely that you encounter a narcissist from certain nations than not. Finding a humble person in certain nationalities is like discovering rare treasure. That's because the spirit of narcissism is a familiar spirit and a principality to that nation. Narcissism is rooted in pride. Wherever there is pride there will be rebellion, witchcraft, or pagan practices; iniquity, and idolatry. The idol that narcissists worship is "self." Narcissists think more highly of themselves than they ought, and they love and worship themselves. Such nationalities tend to be highly atheistic. The minority that believes in God tend to lean towards pagan beliefs that cuddles them with illusions of grandeur. If someone moves to that nation or become friends with a group of people from that nation, that spirit of narcissism can become familiar to that person, and they too can become a narcissist. It's not to say that there are no true or humble believers in Christ in such nations, but they are usually in the minority. Revival is a great way to dislodge the principality of such nations.

Other nations can be bound by other familiar spirits and principalities such as spirits of violence, crime, injustice, corruption, poverty, racism, sexual immorality, sexual perversion, and the like.

Some nations are governed by covenant-breaking spirits. In such nations, leaders don't keep their word to the people or to their own team members. This can occur politically and in other spheres of leadership. Also, businesses and organizations will tend not to function with integrity; of course, this dynamic could exist everywhere, but, in such nations, such behaviors are more widespread. The population in general tend to be covenant-breaking in various ways, such as breaking agreements and promises, telling secrets, disclosing confidential information, backstabbing, and deception. Also, there will also be strong evidence of disloyalty between spouses, cheating, and high divorce rates, since these are manifestations of a covenant-breaking spirit. In such nations, a covenant-breaking spirit becomes a familiar spirit to the population.

Race

Rejection and stigmatization are familiar spirits to certain races, especially "minorities." This is not to say that every individual of a minority race carries spirits of rejection or stigmatization. This is also not to say that races that are not "minorities" do not experience rejection and stigmatization. These demons are familiar or have attached themselves to certain races. Often, individuals from such races can be faced with marginalization, outright rejection, racism, stigmatization, and are subjected to being treated with suspicion or accused of having certain behaviors. There are traits, or expectations ascribed to them, or assumptions are made about them with no supporting evidence aside from race. For people of these races, the strategy is, "Give no place to the devil." If your race is treated a certain way because of how they dress, or a certain set of traits are unduly ascribed to it, if you don't want to be rejected or stigmatized, then dress and conduct yourself differently. Dress how you want to be addressed, and demand to be respected when others fail to show respect.

Extend the courtesies that you want to be extended to you. Speak to others in the way that you want others to speak to you. Some things are solved through prayers, and others through practical means. Find practical ways to present yourself well. If you don't want to be treated like a gangster, do not look or speak like a gangster. If you don't want to be treated with suspicion, do not behave suspiciously. Sometimes, people just match your energy, while others are racist. Recognize the difference.

Secondly, take control of your mind. Self-control is soul control; master the mind. Control how you think, feel and respond. You don't need to react to every racist. If you do, you will build into your sub-conscious mind an unnecessary sensitivity to racism, or an unnecessary discomfort, suspicion, and assumption about certain races. Learn to relax, learn to ignore, learn to let things go and be the bigger person. If something gets out of control, then you nip it in the bud. Don't go into situations expecting to be rejected or stigmatized. Situations tend to match our expectations.

Thirdly, if you experience racism and stigmatization consistently, you will need to break the agreement in the name of Jesus Christ on a conscious, unconscious, and subconscious level. Cut all ties with the demon of anti .... (whatever your race is) that's trying to become familiar with you.

Lastly, and more importantly, remember that you were created by God, in His image. You reflect an image of God. To be a reflection of God's image is a status, a state of being. All races came from Adam. Hence, all races were created equally. Racism and racial construct were set up by evil men who wanted to feel superior to others. You don't have to buy into their narrative or subscribe to anyone's fake sense of superiority.

God created you; you are loved and accepted by Him. If God can love and accept you, then you are lovable and acceptable first by you. We should never lay the responsibility of feeling loved or accepted at the feet of others without first laying it at our own feet. Love and accept yourself. When you learn to love and accept yourself in a healthy way, it will not matter who does not love or accept you.

One day, Holy Spirit told me, "Self-acceptance is one of the highest forms of worship." I was not struggling with rejection nor dealing with racism. I was just going through the process of being my authentic self and Holy Spirit was encouraging me along. Psalm 139:14 lets us know that we are fearfully and wonderfully made. When we agree with God in this regard, God sees our agreement as worship. God does not want us to discount ourselves because of our race, height, hair type, gender, or anything else. He loves us and He wants us to love ourselves. Rejection, racism, stigmatization and the like are constructs that came straight out of hell; they did not come from the throne of God.

"Sole" Ties

Yes, you read correctly; I did not make a mistake. Familiar spirits can cause a person to become sole-tied to a place. One time I was interceding for someone. God showed me this person's feet had something like lead attached to them. His feet were extremely heavy, and he could hardly lift them up to walk. God then instructed me to break the sole tie between him and that place. God wanted to move this man out of that place, but a bondage existed between the soles of his feet and the ground. Because his feet were like lead, gravity had the advantage. His mind, for whatever reason, felt a sense of obligation and commitment to that place and the people there, so he became grounded. God wanted to free him of it.

Sometimes this soul tie to familiar spirits can exist subliminally; so, the agreement is not deliberate, yet the bond exists in the subconscious or unconscious mind, under the radar of the conscious mind. Hence, we do not do certain things intentionally, yet for some reason there seems to be a natural propensity to think or act a certain way, or we are drawn to certain practices or objects. Whether the soul tie exists with an individual agreement or subliminally, it explains why some people are in church for many years but struggle to reach their full potential in God, or in life. The familiar spirits tie them to a threshold and to certain patterns.

ALTARS

My original intention was to write a prayer specifically addressing altars, but I realized that altars can be complex and vary from situation to situation. Hence, I may not be able to write a prayer that's broad enough or specific enough. It's better if I explain what an altar is and advise you how to address it effectively.

We all have altars, whether they were built deliberately or not. An altar is a place where sacrifices are offered to a deity. There are altars to the Most High, and there are altars to fallen deities. There are family altars, and altars that can be built on an individual level. Altars can be erected inside homes, or within public gathering places. Some altars are visible, while some are invisible; visible altars are usually made of wood and stone. Whether visible or invisible, all altars function as points of connection between the natural and spiritual worlds.

An invisible altar can be formed if the same act of worship is repeated in a specific place to a specific deity over a period of time. For example, if I worship the Most High in my home consistently, an altar is established to Him automatically. Hence, my home will become the domain of the Most High. On the other hand, a home or place can become the domain or dwelling place of demons if acts of immorality and iniquity are committed consistently in those places. Different acts of immorality and iniquity fall under different deities; as a result, some places have multiple altars.

How Was It Built?

While we build altars because of whom we worship, we inherit some altars because of whom our ancestors worshipped. If they did not worship the Most High, those altars will need to be torn down. We encounter some altars by proximity. For example, if you move into a house or apartment in which someone was a satanist, a Hindu, practiced New Age, a witch, or the previous occupant was sexually immoral (the bed is an altar), even if these previous occupants had physical altars and took those altars with them when they moved, an invisible altar will be established in that home because life is more spiritual than physical. When those individuals move to a new place, they will have to work to reestablish an atmosphere or spiritual climate. In the meantime, they left one that was already established. It will be your task to demolish that altar and claim that territory.

My Experience

One time I moved to a place that was owned by a Christian. Every time I went to sleep in the bedroom, I felt as though I was being watched. It was very uncomfortable. I asked the owner who was the occupant before I moved in, and the reply was, "It was just a lady." I asked was she religious in any way? The reply was "No." But this feeling of being watched from a specific corner in this bedroom would not go away. Also, I began to experience sleep apnea. I bound, loosed, and the whole nine yards. Then one day the Lord opened my eyes, and I saw, in the spirit, this huge demon or deity—I am unsure which it was—but it was standing in that same corner of the room from which I always felt as though I was being watched. The demon was dressed like an ancient warrior, with a type of a metallic armor.

I asked the owner the same question two more times, "Who lived here before me?" On the third time the reply was, "It was an Indian woman and her son; she was a Hindu." Then I thought, 'There we go.' I asked the Lord, "How do I get rid of this demon?" The Lord told me, "It was worshipped into the home, so you will have to worship it out." That specific spot where that demon/deity stood was the location of the previous tenant's altar. After the Lord told me what to do, I began to worship in my bedroom. When I was not worshipping, I would play worship music. The demon left. It was not immediate. It took weeks to months of doing the same thing consistently. I've always had experiences like this, and I've had to contend with the altar of the previous occupant.

This is why I hate moving.

Do not underestimate people; the ones who may not look like they dabble in anything may be into something. People have their own superstitious beliefs, practices, folklore, and customs which will result in altars being established. Globally, the spiritual climate has heightened. The spiritual and physical realm are more intersected than before; hence altars can be established quickly. This includes technology. Altars can be established by what someone engages consistently via their devices. Those devices can become portals, and black mirrors. What are you sacrificing your time to when you get on your device? Who is influencing you, and who is their deity?

Demonic altars became established through consistent acts of worship to a specific deity. Hence, demonic altars will not be destroyed with one prayer. You will need to swing at it aggressively and consistently to break it down. This approach must be taken whenever you encounter an altar, whether you moved into a place and met it, or you inherited it through your blood-line. Demonic altars need to be addressed because they will speak against your life. Demonic altars are anti-you. Bloodline demonic altars will speak against your life and keep it in negative cycles. The demonic altars that you encounter by way of proximity will create new negative cycles.

You can identify bloodline demonic altars by observing the bloodline and recognizing the deities that your ancestors worshipped. You can identify an altar that you've encountered by observing when something negative started to happen in your life, the life of your spouse, or the lives of your children. It's usually something new, or the return of an old habit or challenge. You can also encounter a demonic altar in your workplace, at schools, at hospitals, and in other public places. Don't attack every altar you encounter. Don't pick unnecessary fights. Some demons are very vicious. It's not that you are afraid; it's just that you may not have the legal right to overthrow an altar. It is important to understand your legal rights in specific spiritual situations.

You have legal rights to address bloodline altars because you are part of that bloodline. In this case you have the legal right to disconnect you and your children from it. You may not have the legal right to tear down altars on behalf of the entire bloodline unless the family asked you to do so. If other members of the family want to maintain their demonic altar, you have no business trying to overthrow their right.

You have legal rights to address altars in places that you occupy because you are the new tenant or the new owner. The ownership document or the lease agreement gives you the legal right. This is the same premise for your job. If you occupy an office space because you were employed or promoted and you were placed in a specific spot, you have the legal right to overthrow previous altars. But don't overthrow altars of the entire company or department unless instructed by the Lord to do so. What you can do instead is to pray for divine protection or command the demons and deities in the environment to be subjected to you in the name of Jesus Christ. Although you may not be able to tear down all altars within a space, you can still exercise dominion over all altars in that space because of Luke 10:19 ESV: *"Behold, I have given you authority to tread on serpents and scorpions, and over all the power of the enemy, and nothing shall hurt you."*

The same goes for schools, hospitals, and public places in general. Companies, businesses, hospitals, and so on, are often dedicated to or are in allegiance with specific deities. Attempting to overthrow altars where you have no legal rights could lead to terrible repercussions - if not to you and your loved ones, then to others in the environment.

Always be conscious of the fact that your authority in a situation is connected to the legal rights that you have in that situation. Therefore, do not overthrow altars 'just because.' Demons know when you have legal rights, and if you don't, they will use their legal rights to retaliate, resist, and afflict you. Besides what I mentioned earlier, legal rights can come with an instruction from God as well. If God tells you to tear down an altar, tear it down. Your legal right is in the instruction.

How to Tear Down an Altar

<u>Fix Your Heart.</u> Purity and holiness are important. You cannot be a lukewarm believer and overthrow altars of any kind. You cannot have iniquity in your heart and break curses of any kind. You cannot break a curse if your lifestyle can be the cause of a curse; you will only increase your trouble. You cannot break altars if you are bitter, hateful, envious, jealous, sexually immoral, or the like. To exercise power and authority, you must walk in purity consistently. I don't mean perfection; I mean purity. We all fall short from time to time. I am referring to habitual sin; believers are not exempt from this. Repent daily.

<u>Identify the Deity or Deities.</u> If you don't know their names, you can identify them by what they are doing or causing to happen. It could be a spirit of death, poverty, strife, divorce, infirmity, or sexual perversion. You can also identify a spirit through the gift of discerning of spirits or word of knowledge. Lean on the Holy Spirit. All altars have both deities and demons. If there was a physical altar, a great way of identifying its former location in the house or apartment is to pinpoint where (what room, corner, etc.) you are harassed demonically the most. Most people tend to keep their altars in their bedrooms or somewhere out of sight because they want to keep it a secret.

<u>Uproot and Tear Down.</u> You destroy an altar by breaking agreement with it and informing the associated deities that you now have legal rights to that space. Exercise your legal right to tear down its altar and evict it in the name of Jesus Christ. Command the deity and associated demons to leave.

<u>Anoint the Space with Oil.</u> Pray over your own oil. Exercise faith and confidence in your relationship with Christ. Stop buying anointing oil. When you buy anointing oil, you open up your life to a sorcerer's anointing. Simon the sorcerer wanted to purchase the power of God with money and received a rebuke instead (refer to Acts 8:9-24). It's better to live under a blessing than under a rebuke. There is no Biblical premise for the sale or purchase of anointing oil. Engaging in this practice makes it witchcraft. You can take the oil to church and ask your leader to pray over it. Anoint your home often. Anoint your office often but be wise and discreet in this regard. Also, in every situation, do not become paranoid.

<u>Follow the Instructions of the Lord.</u> Not all altars are addressed in the same manner. God may have a specific instruction for you like He did with me. Nevertheless, all altars are destroyed in the name of Jesus Christ and by you resisting its attempt to exercise dominion over you. Some situations may be more pesty and you may need to include fasting.

<u>Address Lingering Spirits.</u> Command lingering spirits in a new space to leave. Although a deity may leave, some associated demons may be assigned to linger and monitor, or linger and create an opportunity for the deity to return. When dealing with lingering demons from your bloodline, or ones you attracted on your own, command them to lose your scent and leave. Some demons are predatory in nature; they may back off for a while but track you down by scent and reattach themselves at an opportune time.

Ask the Lord to cleanse and sanctify you according to Ephesians 5:26 so that bloodline demons and demons you attracted on your own can lose your scent. Ask Him to release the fragrance of the Lord upon you. You can also attract fragrance from the presence of the Lord through worship.

<u>Build and Plant - Establish The Lordship of Jesus Christ.</u> Make it known in that place that you are in allegiance with the Most High God. When you overthrow, you must replace. I would say, *"Jesus is my God. He is Lord in this place, and there is none besides Him. He alone rules and reigns, and no spirit that is unlike Him is welcome. Even so Lord Jesus come, be seated, build Your throne here, and establish Your name. Let Your glory be known in this place. Holy Spirit, You are welcome here. I come into agreement with the commandment in Exodus 20:3 ESV that says, "You shall have no other gods before me." I refuse, reject and overthrow every altar built to other gods, in Jesus' mighty name, Amen."*

<u>Dedicate and Sanctify</u> the space unto the Lord and declare it holy ground, whether it's an apartment, a house, a building, or an office space.

<u>Prayer, Praise and Worship Consistently.</u> Doing this will establish your altar to the Lord and drive out other altars. You can also play worship music and the audio Bible. Consistency is key. An altar is a place where you mark a territory as a sign of allegiance to the God that you serve. Praise and extol the Lord with your words. Tell Him that He is good, great and mighty. When this comes directly from you, it is powerful.

<u>Lifestyle.</u> Live a life of obedience to the Lord. Don't be schizophrenic spiritually by confessing one thing but living another. Let your words and your lifestyle agree.

An Unsuspecting Altar

Another way in which an altar can be raised against you in the spirit is through word curses. When someone speaks negatively against your success, progress, or wellbeing deliberately, demons are activated and become attracted to carry out those curses. The constant releasing of word curses can result in an altar of witchcraft being raised against you. If this is not addressed, it will result in failure, stagnation, delay, and a general struggle to progress. People release word curses because of hate, envy, or jealousy. The spirit of jealousy is a gateway spirit. When someone allows jealousy to remain in their heart unchecked, the spirit of jealousy comes and attaches itself to that unchecked trait. This spirit of jealousy then opens the door to spirits of witchcraft, torment, hate, and murder to possess the person that has jealousy. A jealous person is capable of murder. They could unalive or have someone unalive the target of their jealousy. Wherever there is a spirit of jealousy, there will be a spirit of death or murder. *"...Jealousy as cruel as the grave..."* Song of Solomon 8:6 NKJV. This is why you should never trust a jealous person.

In its mild form, the spirit of death or murder manifests itself by way of character assassination and word curses. Both are manifestations of a spirit of witchcraft, but the person with the spirit of jealousy can go deeper into the dark side of witchcraft to have their hate satisfied, hence they may turn to different forms of magic or spells. Jealous people also experience deep mental torment. This is why they torment those around them and display obsessive behaviors.

There is a strong spirit of witchcraft in the Church. It's now bolder and more blatant than before, and this spirit of witchcraft in the church is on many five-fold leaders. It's becoming more and more common to hear Christian leaders both on and off social media uttering word curses on members who left, people they dislike, people they are jealous of and want to see fall, or those who refuse to be controlled by them, or those who disagree with them.

But I am not surprised. A few years ago, the Holy Spirit told me that there will be a mixture between Christianity and witchcraft. This mixture is not restricted to word curses; it will include multiple aspects of witchcraft. Do not sit under a leader who word curses others, because it's only a matter of time before they do it to you. Do not be blinded by charisma, whether online or offline. Many charismatic leaders are very controlling, manipulative, and narcissistic. Narcissists are natural witches. Don't give, tithe, or sow into such people. Don't fund the wicked. When I say 'witch' here, I am referring to both male and female. The male is a warlock, but when I use the word 'witch' I am referring to both.

To overthrow altars of witchcraft raised against you, cancel word curses raised against you and your children daily. Sometimes, people that you don't suspect are cursing you, are indeed cursing you. You, however, have authority over every tongue raised against you in judgment according to Isaiah 54:17 ESV: *"no weapon that is fashioned against you shall succeed, and you shall refute every tongue that rises against you in judgment. This is the heritage of the servants of the LORD and their vindication from me, declares the LORD."* Use that authority.

Secondly, ask God to disappoint those with negative desires and expectations towards you. A curse can also be released this way. And lastly, ask God to cancel every secret counsel that the wicked raised against you because people can gather and agree to attempt to take measures to stagnate your progress or success. That agreement becomes another altar that needs to be torn down.

PRAYER TO RENOUNCE FREEMASONRY

I've added a prayer to renounce freemasonry because some of our ancestors were freemasons.

Prayer

In the name of Jesus Christ, I renounce, refuse, reject, and divorce myself from every covenant that I and my fore-parents, all the way to the 3rd and 4th generations, made with death, Sheol, Lucifer, Lilith, Horus, Baal, deities not mentioned, demons, and familiars, including marine deities and demons both associated and not associated with freemasonry.

I renounce and fall out of agreement with all false communion, and demonic meals. I excuse myself from and fall out of agreement with every demonic table and gathering in every realm. I renounce oaths, vows, covenants, agreements, freemason rituals, and every other ritual, as well as altars, idols, and freemason associations. I renounce and close the third eye. I renounce all forms of ungodly engagement with the Holy Bible. I renounce deities, demons, and familiars associated with freemasonry at every and all levels.

I forsake all involvement in freemasonry by me or my family to the 3rd and 4th generations, and I break every curse, sickness and infirmity, commitment, hindrance, and impediment tied to this involvement. I confess that Jesus is my Lord, and I slam shut every doorway to freemasonry. I renounce all pride, arrogance, control, sorcery, secrecy, witchcraft, poverty and lack, and everything that's associated with freemasonry. I submit to Jesus Christ as my Lord. I come into agreement with the commandment that says, "...have no other gods before me." Deuteronomy 5:7 ESV

I break the power of freemasonry off my life and off my bloodline and I cast aside and out every related and associated spirit and curse off my life and bloodline now. I command every demon associated with freemasonry to come out of my life now, in Jesus' name, Amen.

Finally, I trust that you used this book to reflect prayerfully and recognize the heads of Hydra in your bloodline, in your own life, and in your environment. I trust that you are aware that in the name of Jesus Christ, you have the power to slay the Hydra that you are facing. I trust that you will always remember that you have authority over all—absolutely everything—that is not of God.

Victory is yours, take it!

"Behold, I give you the authority to trample on serpents and scorpions, and over all the power of the enemy, and nothing shall by any means hurt you."
Luke 10:19 NKJV

ABOUT THE AUTHOR

Prophetess Rhonda Crossman is the founder of The Issachar Company, an online Prophetic training hub. She is also an exhaustive Teacher and Preacher of the Gospel of Jesus Christ, and she possesses a passion for purity in the prophetic ministry and in the Kingdom of God as a whole. Rhonda is an avid reader who loves interacting with people from different cultures as well as relaxing at the beach. She is an ordained Prophet and resides with her family in the Netherland Antilles.

References

REFERENCES

Chapter 2

1.CURSE - Definition from the KJV Dictionary. (n.d.). AV1611.com. https://av1611.com/kjbp/kjv-dictionary/curse.html#:~:text=To%20utter%20a%20wish%20of%20evil%20against%20one%3B,mischief%20or%20injury%20to%20fall%20upon%3B%20to%20execrate.

Chapter 4

2.meaning of grind dictionary.com - Bing. (n.d.). Bing. https://www.bing.com/search?q=meaning+of+grind+dictionary.com&form=ANNTH1&refig=0890da6774484d7ab464d85d10276316&pc=LCTS

Chapter 5

3.Wikipedia contributors. (2024a, August 12). *Familiar - Wikipedia*. https://en.wikipedia.org/wiki/Familiar

Chapter 6

4.Wikipedia contributors. (2024, August 25). *Sympathetic magic*. Wikipedia. https://en.wikipedia.org/wiki/Sympathetic_magic

5.Law of contact (Wikipedia) – See Chapter 6, Reference 4

6.Law of similarity (Wikipedia) – See Chapter 6, Reference 4

Chapter 7

7.Solis, M. (2023, November 27). What are teraphim? - Answer The Bible. *Answer The Bible*. https://www.answerthe-bible.com/what-are-teraphim/